Prairie Wanderings

The Land and Creatures
of the Grasslands

Prairie Wanderings

The Land and Creatures
of the Grasslands

Paul G. Jantzen
illustrated by
Kristin Ediger-Goering

Hearth
PUBLISHING

A Division of Multi Business Press
Hillsboro, Kansas

Printed in the United States of America
by Multi Business Press, Hillsboro, KS

Publisher's Cataloging in Publication
    (Prepared by Quality Books Inc.)
Jantzen, Paul G.
    Prairie wanderings: the land and creatures of the grasslands / Paul Jantzen.
    p. cm.
    Includes bibliographical references.
    Preassigned LCCN: 93-79794.
    ISBN 1-882420-05-5
1. Prairie ecology–Great Plains. 2. Prairie flora--Great Plains. 3. Prairie fauna--Great
Plains. 4. Natural history--Great Plains.   I. Title.

QH541.5.P7I35 1993   574.5'2643'0978
                                       QBI93-21686

Contents

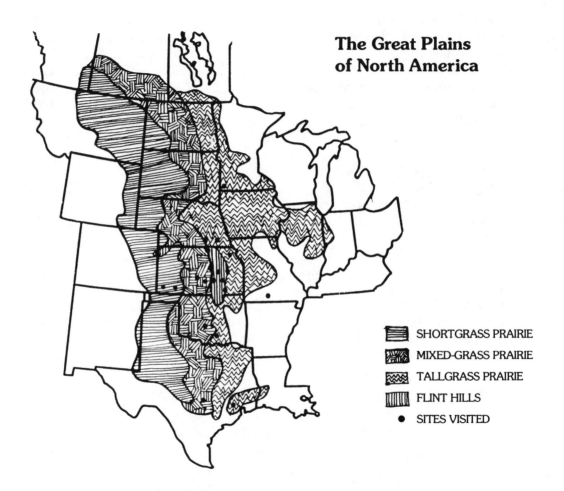

**The Great Plains
of North America**

SHORTGRASS PRAIRIE
MIXED-GRASS PRAIRIE
TALLGRASS PRAIRIE
FLINT HILLS
● SITES VISITED

Foreword

To create this book, Paul Jantzen has gathered a delightful collection of his natural history essays, gleaned from personal experiences and observations since the 1950s. Many of his articles were adapted from early letters to his mother, in which he shared with her his views and ideas. Their love of woodlands and prairies was mutual. Later in his career, he incorporated many of his compositions into a popular nature column for the *Hillsboro Star-Journal*, his hometown newspaper.

Paul is a biologist in the broadest sense. His writings are not so much about specific creatures or land forms or wildlife phenomena as they are about the diverse interrelationships of the natural world. His chapters suggest this immediately—*Origin of the Prairie, Feathered Entomologists, Mulberries and Silkworms*, or *Tragedy Along the South Ninnescah*. Not for him the cloistered, narrow view, but instead the all-inclusive splendor of seeing nature at large, always floating and shifting between harmony and discord, yet resilient and compelling to an observant visitor.

Read this book at ease. Read it when you settle down on a cold winter's night, or beneath a friendly shade tree at mid-summer. Think about what you read. And go out and try to retrace the steps of its author and see what he has seen. You will be richer for it, and your increased wealth will be reward enough for Paul. Much of his soul is in this book, revealing his lifelong commitment to nature and her ways. He wants you to experience it, too.

I have known Paul for many years and treasure him as a friend and colleague. He is well-known nationally as a biology teacher, having co-authored both *Macmillan Biology* and *Macmillan Life Science* in the 1980s. He also served a term as president of the *Kansas Association of Biology Teachers*, and was their editor for fourteen years. Although now retired from formal teaching, he continues to learn and observe and write from his home in Hillsboro, Kansas. Take your copy of this book and visit him. Get an autograph. Better yet, get a story from him about the natural world around you. It will profit you much.

Joseph T. Collins
Lawrence, Kansas
19 July 1993

Preface

My mother loved the woods and prairies. She appreciated her birthplace on a farm in the glaciated area of southeast Nebraska. Here along Cub Creek she and her sisters enjoyed the scenic prairies and woods where they worked and played. Wildflowers and birds were their companions. In her aging years, she was confined to her bed and was no longer able to walk the prairies and woods, or even to reply to my letters. Dialogue with Mother became monologue. Her care-takers would read to her the letters sent by her children. This one-way communication became difficult for me. Yet, separated from all of her children by geography and from her husband by death, she needed to continue hearing from her children.

For a time it became a regular Sunday afternoon activity for me to take a hike partly for my own enjoyment and self-renewal, and partly to provide substance for letters to Mother. A two-hour hike in the public hunting area of the local reservoir, or in the gallery forest along French Creek, or along the Santa Fe Railroad tracks provided enough stimulating observations to fill a few pages of nature ramblings. As a biology teacher, I would tie observations together with what I knew or could easily reach in my library. And I could add any philosophical musings and theological reflections that flowed from this immersion into the natural world.

Later, nearing retirement age, I timidly asked the editor of our local weekly newspaper, *The Hillsboro Star-Journal*, whether her readers would find a nature column useful. I reasoned that my life-long interest in the biosphere might continue to help people understand how the world works, though the "students'" ages would expand beyond that of the teen years. The editor agreed to accept my efforts and the style developed through letters to Mother was applied to producing about two columns of "Prairie Wanderings" per month. Many of the chapters in this collection first appeared in that format.

I share these observations to encourage the readers' appreciation of the living world. Awareness of personal connections with our natural surroundings is a vital step toward establishing a lifestyle that respects the planet that is our home.

I believe that the prairie doesn't have to be made interesting. It is interesting by its very nature. Rather, I have tried to provide a few examples from a vast array of interrelationships that suggest the complexity of the prairie and both its fragility and its resilience.

Of course reading about the prairie isn't enough. Nothing can replace actual walks in the grasslands, personally experiencing the sights, sounds, and smells they offer. I hope these stories encourage readers to do their own prairie wanderings.

The information that I share is gleaned from years of study by many dedicated biologists and ecologists to whom I am in debt. Whether formal mentors, hiking companions, or writers, their names would fill many pages. I thank them all.

I do express special gratitude to several people who made this immediate project possible; Kristin Ediger-Goering for the fine drawings that add visual descriptions to the text, Judy Goering who faithfully transcribed my hodge podge of manuscripts onto a computer disk, Joe Collins for his kind words in the Foreword, Elaine Jantzen who was gracious while I was hiking or writing when she thought other projects had higher priority, and the folks at Hearth Publishing—Joel, Stan, Linda, Marsha, Charity, and others behind the scenes who produced the final product.

SUMMER

A Prairie Vocalist

The bubbling song of the western meadowlark filled the morning air already full of sunlight.

Elaine and I had reached the country church early that Sunday. We took a short walk down the dirt road that stretched between two rows of wooden posts that held several strands of barbed wire. One post had a special task that day. It was the stage for the morning's avian soloist.

The bird's golden breast contrasted with its bold black tie as he sang. The sight, and the song, and the prairie smells were awe-inspiring. That morning, worship began before the congregation arrived.

Others, too, have found the western meadowlark worthy of attention. It is the State Bird of Kansas, Nebraska, North Dakota, Montana, Oregon and Wyoming.

But there are more than melodious notes and golden feathers that determine this bird's success as a prairie species, although both contribute. For one, its food consists of insects and seeds, of which both abound in the grassland. It devours beetles, crickets, grasshoppers, caterpillars, ants, bees, wasps and bugs. Plant foods include wild and domestic grains and sunflower seeds.

Sites and materials for nest construction are abundant. The western meadowlark nests on the ground in dense cover. It builds a loose bowl of grass litter often with a partial dome that hides its white eggs, spotted with browns and purples.

Protecting the meadowlark from an occasional prairie falcon is its camouflaged upper surface streaked with browns that easily blend into the prairie litter. Predators usually view these birds from above as meadowlarks spend much of their time walking or crouching on the ground or in low-altitude flight.

While camouflage may protect the meadowlark from predation, the bird depends on bold colors to establish and maintain territory. Limiting a territory to the use of one breeding pair avoids overpopulation which could exceed the area's carrying capacity.

When challenged, the male displays color patches to rival males. These patches are the bright yellow breast with a black V and the white sides of the tail usually hidden by brown tail feathers.

The competing males point their bills upward and open and close their wings and tail feathers rapidly. They fluff out their bright yellow plumage and make short jump-flights toward each other. Singing from elevated perches while displaying the yellow breast is another expression of territoriality.

A similar behavior is also used by the male meadowlark in courtship. The female may respond similarly without the jump-flights.

Exposing the white sides of the tail also communicates with other meadowlarks during winter flocking. The white flashing probably helps keep the birds together and may warn of possible danger. Such flashing is especially evident during flight and in landing. But it also occurs during ground feeding.

The flocking color signal is common in several small grassland bird species that sometimes form flocks. And the male dickcissel, a prairie finch, is also streaked with brown above and displays a yellow breast with a black V. "How is it," asked ecologist Durward Allen, "that the grassland habitat tends to mold its creatures into certain patterns for their welfare and survival?"

The use of abundant resources for food and nesting, the camouflaging of its upper plumage, and the effective use of color patching in territorial, courtship and flocking behaviors all contribute to the success of the western meadowlark. But the beauty of its feathers and the thrill of its melodious whistle add an aesthetic touch which greatly enhances my appreciation of this common prairie species.

Elm Springs

A blue jay screams in protest as I make my way down the rocky hillside that descends to the spring brook below. The brook originates from springs in the wooded ravine and flows over the open rock surface only to drop into a box canyon filled with American elms, green ash, black walnut and a host of understory shrubs and herbs.

As part of the Smoky Hills Upland, this hilly region was eroded into the Dakota sandstone of Cretaceous age. The sandstone protrudes prominently from some slopes while in others it forms rounded hills clothed with tall prairie grasses below and shorter grasses at their summits. The stream in the valley floor is fed by small spring brooks in the hills and ravines which converge to form marshy areas and, further on, a slow-flowing prairie stream.

Beneath the trees at the lower edge of the wooded ravine, are poison ivy, white avens and Missouri gooseberry. I eat one ripe, dark purple gooseberry and enjoy its sweet taste. I leave the green ones for later meals by brown thrashers, skunks, raccoons, and coyotes.

Between the ravine and the falls, the brook flows over a rocky area devoid of trees, but in which scattered shrubs occur. Ankle deep in water stand broadleaf arrowhead, common bulrushes and agrimony, a rose with small yellow flowers not yet in bloom. Beside the stream, a yellow sulphur butterfly flits among chickasaw plums and goldenrods.

Many of the goldenrods have prominent swellings in their stems—like small snakes that have swallowed large eggs. These swellings, called galls, are caused by the larvae of a fly. This goldenrod gall fly is about six millimeters long with broad zigzag bands on its brown wings. In early summer, the female lays an egg in the tip of the goldenrod. Upon hatching, the young larva bores into the stem and carves out a living chamber. The plant develops the gall in response to the irritation of the larva.

By mid-September, the white, five-millimeter-long larva scrapes an exit tunnel out toward the epidermis. Here it pupates in late April. When the pupa matures, the adult escapes from the gall, mates and continues the cycle.

Before descending into the box canyon, I decide to explore the grassy hillside with its bluffs and boulders of calcite-cemented sandstone. Scattered among the grasses on this slope are white sage, common ragweed, wavyleaf thistle and hoary vervain with its sky-blue flowers. I avoid the stickleaf mentzelia because its leaves are difficult to remove from clothing. Its yellow flowers appear wind-whipped. I see none of the prickly pear cactus I saw here three years ago.

Some of the sandstone surfaces are plastered with blotches of crusty lichens, each composed of a fungus and an alga. Various species are blue-green, gray or a bright greenish yellow.

Tucked in cracks between narrow ledges of sandstone are the small bluish green cloak ferns, about four centimeters long. I had seen them here three years ago and wondered whether they could survive these warm, dry conditions. They did survive! They probably use water stored in sandstone from occasional rains. A pale-seeded plantain grows in the soil accumulated in a cupped depression in the sandstone.

Now I head back to the box canyon to enjoy the shade of the various trees, and the choke cherries, bittersweet, poison ivy vines, water hemlock and black raspberry bushes, all fed by a steady garden-hose-size stream of spring water. The water drops three meters from the rock ledge above, having originated back in the wooded ravine we saw earlier. In this "tropical rain forest," I admire the multitude of blackwing damselflies with their iridescent green abdomens. Their wings are a shining brownish black and are held back over their backs when at rest.

But I need to search for another species of fern I saw here three years ago under a second waterfall hidden by shrubbery in the south wall of this canyon.

I step carefully to avoid slipping in the mud and edge past the falling water into the recess under the falls. And there on the ledges of this dripping-wet cavern are the beautiful bladder ferns! On the same ledges I see the soft, pale-green moss, *Pohlia wahlenbergii*. It is one of the 44 moss species that have been identified in Marion County by bryologist Gary Merrill.

My thoughts are interrupted at this point by the sound of human voices—children's voices. I wait while eight chattering children, seven boys and a girl with a white head covering descend, single-file, to the canyon floor. Following at some distance are the two Amish-Mennonite fathers of the children; Aaron Miller, a local resident for the past year, and Greg Avina of Lamar, Missouri. While the children, with one of the water jugs, go exploring beyond the canyon, the men and I remain in the shade. Our conversation covers cave ecology, theology, faith vs. culture, and the hardships of pioneers. Greg, who has had university training in botany, is interested in the ferns. Bringing their children to romp in the prairie will help them understand their biological roots—their connection with the natural world.

After about an hour, I decide it's time to head for the hills on the other side of the valley. And I will be on the lookout for another fern that biologist Ralph Brooks says is found here.

●   ●   ●

After finding the cloak and bladder ferns on sandstone ledges and under/behind the waterfall, I keep my eyes open for the marsh fern that biologist Ralph Brooks has seen here in the Smoky Hills Upland. Leaving the box canyon, I see American licorice with its prickly brown fruits. In the marsh below the canyon are the mud-loving pale smartweed and broad-leaved cattails. Among the cattails, the redwings sound their gurgling *konk-la-ree*. Back in the canyon, I hear the throaty song of a yellow-billed cuckoo.

On a dry island within the marsh, I see musk thistle! I am too late to remove its flowers. It has already bloomed, its pretty rose-purple head has matured, and its seeds have been dispersed by the wind. In 1932, this European immigrant was known in this state only in Washington County. Now it is considered a noxious weed state-wide. It is certainly a successful species.

5

I slosh through the shallow marsh to the west side of the valley and begin ascension along a deeply eroded cattle trail. Here is a wind-beaten prairie coneflower, its yellow ray flowers looking sad indeed.

A sandstone outcropping on this east-facing slope interrupts the grassland cover. Goldenrods, with galls, American licorice, ironweed, vervain, and a large, gray-leaved buffalo-gourd all surround a now-dead, leaning and twisted black willow. And, in the small marsh are water parsnips impersonating ferns. I had encountered this species in a Stafford County marsh back in 1957.

At this level and below are several marshlands, each with its own mix of cattails, parsnips, bulrushes, and agrimony.

Nearing the summit of the rounded hill, we see only grasses and upland wildflowers. A plains yellow primrose clings to the hillside. A grasshopper sparrow flits over the grasses and drops suddenly out of sight. Common St. John's-wort attracts my attention. The dark red specks on its yellow petals reminded early botanists of St. John's blood. White prairie-clover holds up its clean, dainty blossoms. The gray-leaved lead plant, whose roots reach meters into the soil, displays its stalk of light blue flowers.

To reach the highest hill, I must pass through another marsh filled with agrimony and cattails. Nearby are buckbrush, wild bergamot, a narrow-leaved milkweed, mourning doves, dickcissels, and a brown thrasher. I spot a sensitive briar, its rose-pink flowers already matured. I can't resist; I press a leaf between my thumb and forefinger, release it, and watch the leaflets fold. So ruffled by me, or the wind, or some predator, the drooping plant may be less tempting to a grazing animal.

Now on the highest summit, I see the grasses sharing space with two soil-enriching legumes, lead plant and scurf-pea. The first time I mounted this rounded summit, I noted a black swallowtail butterfly barely able to maneuver its frame in the wind as it flew from flower to flower. If there is a breeze anywhere in sight it would be felt up here. The few purple coneflowers have already lost their pink-to-purple ray flowers to the wind.

The nearby wildflowers and butterflies, and the more distant green, rounded hills and gentle valleys remind me of Maria in *The Sound of Music* as she frolicked through the Alpine meadows singing "The hills are alive..." This is really a worship experience!

From aloft, I can see the course of the valley stream and am anxious to observe its life before heading home. At the stream's edge, among the water parsnips, are water hemlocks, described as the "most poisonous of all flowering plants."

In the stream, shaded by a mulberry tree, are the protruding heads of a dozen turtles, probably western painted turtles. They eat both plant and animal matter, dead or alive.

Along the open stream in the low shrubbery are wood nymph butterflies. Each forewing displays two dark circles against a yellow background. The larvae eat grasses. The adults visit flowers but prefer tree sap and decaying fruits for food. A duck skims behind the tops of shrubs to a spot upstream. A dickcissel sings and I see the knee-high Indian plantain standing stiff. But there are no marsh ferns in sight!

A few cattle seem interested in my wanderings. The water supply in this valley once made this a favorite stopping place along the Chisolm Trail. Beginning in 1868, it served as a common route for moving cattle from Texas to the railroad at Abilene, a two-day drive further north. After a rest in this tranquil valley, the cattle looked fresh when they reached Abilene.

At the exit gate, a chickasaw plum provides a few ripe red fruits. Exactly 146 years and two days ago, newly-wed Susan Magoffin stopped at Cottonwood Point along the Santa Fe Trail eight miles southeast of here, and ate gooseberries, raspberries, and a green wild plum. The plums are early this year.

Near the gate, labelled "Elm Springs," are the low-growing puncture vines and, along the fence, buffalo burs. As I head home, a red-headed woodpecker flies along the sandy road and a turkey vulture glides on convection currents generated by the sun that provides energy for all us prairie creatures.

The Purple Poppy Mallow

During a dry, hot day on the prairie, a refreshing sight is the striking blossom of the purple poppy mallow. From May through September you are likely to find its magenta-red petals forming an open cup a little larger than a human thumb nail. The five petals are white at the base and attach to the tubular collection of pollen-bearing stamens which surround the styles of the female flower parts.

This mallow is low-lying and somewhat vinelike, producing deeply incised leaves. The deep incisions reduce surface area which prevents water loss from drying winds. The earlier spring leaves have shallower incisions. Food manufactured in the leaves is stored in the thickened taproot. These drought-resistant qualities assure the poppy mallow's existence in the west three-fourths of Kansas and on west to Utah. Its range extends from northern Texas barely into North Dakota and Minnesota.

The starchy root may be eaten raw in late summer and fall, or fried in butter. The Osage Indians stored the roots in caches for winter eating. In spring and summer the leaves may be cooked and used to thicken soup. It is closely related to the domestic okra whose pods are used for the same purpose. Another relative is the marshmallow, introduced in the eastern U.S. from Europe. Its root yielded the original marshmallow paste which is now replaced by a synthetic preparation in making the popular puffy confection.

The Indian names for the purple poppy mallow referred to its medicinal uses. Indians boiled the roots and drank the liquid for intestinal pains. They burned the dried roots and inhaled their smoke for head and bronchial colds.

The official name of purple poppy mallow is *Callirhoe involucrata*. The genus name, *Callirhoe*, is the name of a beautiful ocean nymph in Greek mythology. The specific name is from the Latin *involucrum* which means wrapper. It refers to the extra three narrow bracts attached to the underside of each flower.

Next time you walk across the prairie, look for the purple poppy mallow, taste its root, remember its history, and drink its beauty.

Origin of the Prairie

The Wilbur and Rhoda Broadie Prairie Reserve couldn't be prettier. Here on the western edge of the Flint Hills in Cowley County, three miles east of the Walnut River, this land is being dedicated this morning as a natural area for use in ecological education and research. In memory of her parents, Wanda Broadie Alexander is donating the land to Bethel College for preservation management. Among the emerging tall grasses, the blue false indigo and western yarrow are in full bloom. And so are many other species.

Eighteen years ago (1975 May 10), I was 430 km (270 miles) straight west of this tallgrass prairie at the Cimarron National Grasslands. There the grasses are shorter, even in mid-spring. And the wildflowers blooming in the two prairies differ. Here in the east, purple poppy mallow is common. In the west, the scarlet globe mallow displays its salmon blossoms among the short buffalo and blue gramma grasses.

Even the geologic origin of surface features differ. The surface here is of Permian age, sea deposits more than 250 million years old. In the west, wind-laid deposits of Quaternary age are exposed. They originated less than two million years ago.

Geologic strata in Kansas slope downward toward the west while the surface slopes upward. So as one proceeds westward, progressively younger strata appear at the surface. The sequence of those rock layers and the fossils embedded in them suggest the history of the American Midwest.

The earliest signs of life in the Great Plains today originated 500 million years ago when the land was flooded and the sea deposited layers of limestone which contain a great variety of fossils of once-living creatures. During the next 450 million years, alternate invasions and recessions of waters left alternating layers of limestone and shale. During recessions, erosion removed some layers, the eroded surface being covered by deposits of succeeding invasions.

A dominant feature of Permian outcroppings in the Flint Hills is the hard limestone with interbedded chert (flint) strata. These erosion-resistant layers form ridges with east-facing slopes.

Layers of coal formed 300 million years ago suggest that the climate for a time was warm and humid. Tree ferns and giant horsetails flourished on the land. From 240 million to 63 million years ago dinosaurs appeared and flourished for a time, and then disappeared. Grasses became common. And Earth's single great land mass was breaking up into the separate continents we know today. As this Age of Reptiles came to a close, the Rocky Mountains pushed up from the land.

Sands and gravels flushed down from the Rockies were deposited on the western Great Plains and further east along rivers. But more important to the formation of prairie than this erosive action, was the climate change brought about by the continued uplifting of the Rocky Mountains. As the jet stream moved moist air from the Pacific Ocean east across the land, the air was pushed up the windward slope of the Rockies. With decreasing pressure from above, the rising air expanded and cooled. The cool air, less able to hold its moisture, dropped it as rain or snow.

On the leeward side of the mountains the air, now wrung dry, provided little rainfall and low humidity. With insufficient moisture to sustain trees, the forests disappeared, leaving the shortgrasses to dominate the plains of eastern Colorado and western Kansas.

Further east, the warm dry air was influenced by the northerly flow of moist air from the Gulf of Mexico. The increased rainfall and higher humidity made possible by Gulf moisture generated the mid-grass and tallgrass prairies characteristic of eastern portions of the Great Plains. Still further east, more directly north of the Gulf, increased Gulf moisture supported deciduous forests. Precipitation gradient across Kansas ranges from 40.6 cm (16 in) per year in the west to 106.7 cm (42 in) in the southeast.

From 25 million years ago until the period of glaciation, much of the Great Plains resembled the African savanna. The plains were largely grassland with an abundance of shrubs and a few scattered trees. Woodlands existed mostly along streams.

About two million years ago, weather changes in the Northern Hemisphere ushered in a series of four glacial invasions. These ice sheets originated in Canada and crept southward, the second one reaching into northeast Kansas. As the ice flowed southward, it scooped out valleys, dozed in rock debris, and brought cold, moist climate to the plains. Canadian spruce forests and oak woodlands invaded the prairies.

With the formation of the great ice sheets came the lowering of the sea level due to the interruption of the water cycle. Water evaporating from the oceans and converted to snow and glacial ice returned to the sea only after the eventual melting of glaciers. While sea water existed as glaciers, the sea level dropped sufficiently to expose the sea floor between Alaska and Siberia. Across this dryland bridge, migrated many species. The modern horse walked to Asia and on to Europe and Africa. (Horses were returned to their native Americas by Spanish explorers in the 1500s.) Ancestors of the American bison crossed the land bridge from Asia to Alaska, followed by the human immigrants that became Eskimos and Indians. Humans moved south along the east slope of the Rocky Mountains as early as 12,000 years ago and witnessed glacial melting and the re-establishment of mid-continent grasslands.

So this Broadie Prairie Reserve is the culmination of millions of years of geologic, climatologic, and biologic change. Its preservation will allow human observers to study continued changes in an area that experiences a minimum of direct human interference. We need this information to serve as a standard by which we can measure the increasing effects of human activity on the health of our planet.

Sand Castles of the Prairie

The large reddish-brown ant plucked a seed from the top of a pigweed, ran down the stem, and scurried across the clearing to the gravel-covered mound nearby. It headed straight for an entrance at the southwest edge of the mound and disappeared inside.

The round-topped mound was 30 centimeters high and a meter wide at its base. The surrounding ground was clear of vegetation forming a bare circle ranging from one to two meters out from the mound.

This mound is the home and granary of the western harvester ant. And farmers, just weeks ago, passed it by to transport their grain to more distant storage facilities.

Inside the mound's entrance is a lobby from which tunnels lead into an extensive multi-level system of chambers and connecting channels reaching two to three meters underground. Some of the chambers store seeds collected by these agricultural ants.

The surface of the mound is made of gravel and soil cemented together to make a nearly waterproof shell. Where gravel is not available, cinders, lava, broken glass, or even tiny fossils are collected from the ground surface. An ant may bring pieces up to 30 times its own weight. But usually the largest granules carried are no longer than the ants themselves, that is about seven millimeters.

The fossil-collecting activity of harvester ants was discovered a century ago in the Wyoming badlands. Now, Kansas University paleontologist Larry Martin says that use of these insects is "like having literally thousands of little workers in your employ..." In a few days, sifting through a dozen ant mounds netted him 7,000 fossil teeth and jaws of small prehistoric mammals.

This volume of fossil material may provide answers to some of paleontology's exciting questions. Was climate change involved in the extinction of dinosaurs? Do species change slowly through time, or in periodic sudden spurts?

Western harvester ants are found generally west of the Mississippi River. In Kansas, they are found in the western two-thirds of the state. But their fossil collecting occurs only where fossils are small and present at Earth's surface. Skimming a two to three centimeter layer from the cone without damaging larval chambers makes collection from the same mounds possible every two to three years.

Paleontologists call this species of ant "Pogo" from its official name, *Pogonomyrmex occidentalis.*

The queen and adult workers spend the winter below frost line in an inactive, non-feeding state. During summers, the upper chambers serve as hatchery, nursery and living quarters of the queen and workers. The cone-shaped surface of the mound receives direct rays of the sun in spring and fall and twice the energy absorption as that of nearby level surfaces. The higher temperatures within the cone shorten incubation times of ant eggs and larvae.

Ecologists have considered possible advantages of the circle of bare soil kept clear by the ants. One advantage is the faster drying of the area after rains. Another is the lack of fuel for possible prairie fires. Diverting the fire from the mound would protect ants and stored seeds from heat damage.

Our harvester ants gather seeds from a variety of plants. They include pigweed, goosefoot, prickly poppy, goldenaster and a number of grasses. They pluck ripened seeds from the plant or search the ground for fallen seeds. A large colony can harvest two cups of seeds per day. For protein supplements they also collect some dead insects and bird droppings.

Before storage, the workers remove the hull of the seed and nip the tip of the embryonic root. This usually prevents sprouting of the seed during storage. Seeds are organized according to kind and stored separately. Following heavy rains, dampened seeds are spread out in the sun to dry to avoid molding.

Sometimes the seeds lost, discarded or forgotten sprout and grow near the mound. Since this growth corresponds to the plants most favored by the ants, early observers believed that ant workers deliberately planted the seeds, an agricultural practice which proved to be a fable.

In mid to late summer, the well-fed males and queens develop wings for their mating flight, During swarming, the ants are often devoured by the open mouths of flying swallows, kingbirds and nighthawks.

But always a few survive to populate those mysterious sand castles of the open prairie.

The Purple Coneflower, Pharmacy of the Prairie

In June and early July, I enjoy the knee-high purple coneflowers that stand erect, well above the prairie grasses of early summer. Unlike its sunflower relatives, this coneflower has drooping ray flowers that are light pink to light purple, arranged around a prickly knob of crowded dark brown scales and somewhat shorter disc flowers. Each head of flowers is born on its own stalk that arises from a thick black perennial root.

The ray flowers are sterile; but the disc flowers mature into four-angled fruits about a half centimeter long. The ray flowers may last a month but the dark central cone remains conspicuous until late autumn. Black Sampson is another common name for this prairie species.

The species' technical name is *Echinacea angustifolia* from the Greek *echinos* (hedgehog) in reference to its prickly knob, and the Latin *angustus* (narrow) and *folium* (leaf) for its narrow leaves.

This handsome coneflower may be seen on rocky slopes and upland prairies and plains in most of Kansas and beyond. Since it is nutritious and eaten by all kinds of livestock, it decreases in numbers in overgrazed grassland. It appears to be drought-hardy; it may even increase in numbers during periods of drought.

To test one of its reported properties, I chewed a bit of its black woody root. A tingling sensation and thorough numbing of my tongue and mouth convinced me of its value. No wonder the Plains Indians placed pieces of its root against an aching tooth for relief. Burns were bathed in the plant's juices to alleviate pain. And to impress observers, some Indians bathed their hands and arms in the plant's juices so they could remove a piece of meat from a boiling kettle with bare hands without suffering pain. One used the plant to so desensitize his mouth to heat that he could hold a live coal in his mouth to the marvel of his audience.

But there must have been other effects. Echinacea was widely used as an antidote for bites of poisonous snakes and insects. It was used in the treatment of headache, enlarged glands (mumps), sore throat, stomach cramps and fits. Among the Plains Indians, it "was used as a remedy for more ailments than any other plant," according to Melvin Gilmore who interviewed many elderly Indians early in this century.

It wasn't only the Indians that saw value in the species. By 1852, European invaders were using it medicinally. In 1885, a Pawnee City, Nebraska, physician introduced an extract of Echinacea called Meyer's Blood Purifier. He claimed it to be a cure for tumors, syphilis, ulcers, typhus and other ailments. In 1887, a Cincinnati pharmaceutical firm began marketing a similar product which was widely used for several decades. From 1916 to 1950, the plant was included in the *National Formulary*, a kind of official list of plants and other substances with medical value.

In recent years, interest in medicinal uses of this coneflower has revived, the dried roots again being purchased by pharmaceutical firms. Modern research methods are applied to re-examine a variety of therapeutic properties such as antibiotic activity, acceleration of wound healing, allergy relief, stimulation of the immune system, growth inhibition of some cancers, and resistance to viral infections.

This revival of interest in the purple coneflower for research and current interest in wild-crafting has botanists worried that over-collection may endanger the survival of this pharmacy of the prairie.

Feathered Entomologists

The hungry chattering of fledgling barn swallows echoed from a half-cup mud nest plastered against the roof beam of a small shelterhouse. It was Sunday morning in late June of 1977 at a private campground in Harvey County. I had been asked to share in the worship service directing our attention to "God's Creation." Making the point that "humankind is ultimately as subject to the laws of nature as is the most helpless creature in the prairie," I pointed to the young swallows above me.

For centuries, barn swallows have built their nests of mud and grasses, attaching them to rocks under overhanging ledges, or in caves and crevices. With the arrival of European settlers, the swallows discovered better protection from weather extremes in human-made structures. Open-doored barns and other farm buildings are favorite nesting sites. Esther Lindteigen reported nest building in Velda Hiebert's front porch. This summer, barn swallows built a nest on a wall that directs girls from the community swimming pool to their dressing room. Up to 20 nests have been counted just below the ceilings of the large concrete culverts associated with the highways that cross the Midwest prairies. There is even record of barn swallows raising successful broods in nests on moving ferry boats. Ornithologists believe that the increased number of potential nesting sites provided by human constructions has made the species much more abundant.

In these nests of mud and grasses, lined with feathers, the female barn swallow deposits three to six white eggs spotted with reddish brown or purple. The whole drama of family-raising is a public affair, taking place in plain sight of their human neighbors.

Like most swallows, barn swallows eat primarily insects. Most are captured on the wing, the birds flying with open mouths at times and places frequented by insects. The insects eaten most commonly are various beetles, winged ants, bees, wasps, bugs, moths and dragonflies.

The barn swallows of North America winter in Central and South America, Costa Rica and Venezuela, even as far south as Argentina. Many follow coastlines and rivers and the West Indies chain of islands to Venezuela. Unlike most land birds, barn swallows migrate by day.

These birds return to the Midwest in late April. The adults generally return to the same nest site while their offspring establish their own breeding territories elsewhere.

The swallow family also includes the purple martin, and cliff, tree, rough-winged and bank swallows. Only the barn swallow has the deeply forked tail and white tail spots. The similar cliff swallow has a square tail, a white forehead, a buffy rump and builds gourd- or jug-like nests cemented to cliffs or the outside of barns.

The American Dog Tick

Anyone wandering across the Midwest prairie is likely to encounter chiggers and ticks. While chiggers are less likely to be seen than felt, ticks are large enough to be seen as they ascend either one's clothing or the body itself.

Kansas has three kinds of ticks that attack humans. Others suck blood from other mammals, or birds and reptiles. Like chiggers and spiders, ticks are arachnids, relatives of insects.

Probably the most common tick in Kansas is the hard-bodied American dog tick, *Dermacentor variabilis*. It is widely distributed throughout the United States east of the Rocky Mountains. This species is found primarily in the fields and prairies of Kansas, but may also be found in wooded areas and stream banks.

These ticks go through four stages in their life cycle: egg, larva, nymph, adult. It is the adult of this species that attacks humankind. The adults become active in mid-April, multiply until June, and wane in numbers in September. They are about four millimeters long and three millimeters wide. When engorged with blood, they may expand to 10 x 15 mm.

According to Keith Waddington of Kansas' Biological Survey, this tick has a three-host life cycle. After each feeding, the tick drops to the ground, sheds its skin and seeks another animal host.

The adult female, one to eight weeks after feeding, deposits masses of white eggs on the ground. The eggs incubate for one or two months and then hatch into tiny larvae. The six-legged larvae remain on the soil or low vegetation awaiting suitable hosts. Larvae that find suitable small mammal hosts such as meadow mice, white-footed mice or cottontails, attach firmly to the neck or shoulders of the animal. The larva pierces the host's skin and sucks blood for about four days. When engorged, the larva detaches from the host, falls to the ground and finds a protected location in the litter to molt and change into the nymphal stage, a sequence that takes about 10 days. Larvae have been known to live up to 540 days without feeding while awaiting a host.

These eight-legged nymphs are inactive for at least four days and then wait for another small mammal host to brush past. Those finding a host, feed for about six days before falling to the ground and molting again. Nymphs have survived for over 275 days without a meal. After becoming adult, the tick ascends tall vegetation and awaits an appropriate host. Hosts preferred by adults include larger mammals such as white-tailed deer, red foxes, dogs, coyotes, horses and humans. Adult ticks may survive more than two years of starvation awaiting one of these hosts. My quick scraping off of a tick deprives it of a very important meal.

The adults of both sexes feed for a number of days before meeting on the host and mating. The polygamous males may feed after each of several matings. The monogamous females feed for 10 days after a single mating before dropping from the host.

Human skin, being nearly bare, is a convenient target for the adult tick. After piercing the skin, the tick sucks blood. Saliva secreted into the tissue near the mouthparts prevents the coagulation of blood.

Waddington warns that ticks may transmit pathogenic organisms with their bites. While this may not occur often, tularemia, Rocky Mountain spotted fever and relapsing fever can be fatal. Suspected cases should be checked by a physician. The bites of female American dog or lone star ticks occasionally cause tick paralysis in wild animals, livestock and people. It can be fatal if untreated. (The lone-star tick attacks humans in all three active stages of its life cycle.) Only *Ornithodoros turicata*, which has no common name, transmits the relapsing fever bacterium in Kansas. The tick-transmitted lyme disease organism is not yet reported here according to local officials. But 16 cases have occurred in this state during the first half of this year, 1993.

Dead Man's Oak

Dead Man's Oak stood as a sentinel on the bluff overlooking Cub Creek just across the fence from my grandparents' farm in southeastern Nebraska. Its massive trunk gave rise to coarse horizontal limbs which, according to legend, sheltered the grave of an Indian chief.

Regardless of the authenticity of the story, this sturdy bur oak inspired a sense of history in my boyhood imagination.

Bur oaks have contested possession of the land with prairie grasses for centuries. During the signing of the U.S. Constitution some of the Midwest's bur oaks were already old trees. In 1937, along the Marais des Cygnes River in Kansas' Miami County, loggers felled an old bur oak with 303 growth rings. An additional unknown number of rings at the center had already decayed.

Oaks produce one of the most recognizable tree fruits, the acorn. Technically, acorns are nuts. They develop from the female flower after fertilization by pollen from separate male flowers on the same tree or its nearby neighbors. Both flowers appear in late April as or shortly before the leaves appear. Male catkins seven to ten centimeters long hang from the base of new growth or the tip of old growth. Female flowers about two millimeters long develop at the base of leaves on new growth in clusters of one to four.

Bur oak acorns mature by October. The heavily fringed cup is gray and usually encloses half or more of the nut which is 2.5 to 3.5 cm in diameter. The larger fruit provides its specific name, *Quercus macrocarpa*. The nuts drop in fall and usually germinate soon after falling. A tap root descends 18 to 23 cm before new leaves unfold. The extensive root system compensates for the low water content of prairie soils.

If germination does not occur promptly, acorns are likely to rot or be consumed by various animals. They are one of the country's most important wildlife foods. Pheasants and prairie chickens enjoy eating acorns as well as oak buds. Wild turkeys devour whole acorns of some oak species. Deer and elk eat acorns and browse on bur oak twigs and foliage. Chipmunks, squirrels and blue jays store acorns for off-season use.

Acorns were also a common food among Native Americans. They are a good source of protein, magnesium and phosphorus. Their high tannin content, however, gives them a bitter taste and decreases their digestibility. The Indians had various ways of extracting the bitter tannin. Leaching can be accomplished quickly by boiling the nuts for two or more hours, changing water each time it turns brown or yellow. Wildfood enthusiasts have many simple recipes for various acorn preparations: flour, mush, soup, cakes, breads, pancakes and cookies.

In Kansas, two towns were named after the bur oak. A settlement along White Creek in Jewell County was named, simply, "Bur Oak."

A grove of bur oaks in Morris County provided the name of another Kansas town. The 1825 U.S. Congress authorized negotiations with the Osage Indians to allow the marking of a road from Missouri to Santa Fe, New Mexico. Negotiators met in an oak grove along the Neosho River where wagon trains often camped, restocked supplies and used bur oaks to repair wagons before moving on west. The settlement was named "Council Grove." And the bur oak that shaded the signing dignitaries was called "Council Oak." The two-meter stump of this oak is preserved as a landmark commemorating the birthplace of the Santa Fe Trail.

Nearby is another large bur oak with a cache at its base. Here wagon trains and freight caravans left messages for trains and caravans that followed. This tree, the "Post Office Oak," served trains and caravans from 1825 to 1847.

In 1987, middle and high school students planted bur oak acorns in the local city park in observance of the bicentennial of the writing of the U.S. Constitution. The oaks were to be marked as special bicentennial trees.

The acorns, however, disappeared. The park groundsman reported seeing ground squirrels making off with the seeds.

To replace the missing seeds, bur oak seedlings that developed from acorns produced in 1987 were transplanted from the Donahue Hayhook Ranch near Lincolnville in eastern Marion County. Those that survive will provide a living legacy through their longevity, their hardiness and their utilitarian value as shade, ornamental and nut-bearing trees.

Reconstructing the Recent Past

When Ruth Unrau wrote *Who Needs an Oil Well?* in 1968, she remarked that "you need to know an amazing amount about plants and animals just to have a boy run across the pasture." The setting was along the Verdigris River in northeastern Oklahoma in 1932. How did she know which plants and animals existed in the Oklahoma prairies 36 years earlier?

Ruth searched the literature and visited the area personally to answer that question. She assumed that the natural vegetation had not changed much in that time.

Older folks can remember how things were. I remember the landscape of Lonesome Ridge School in Nebraska where I studied for eight years. The slope dropping down to the creek had patches of smooth sumac, wild plum, and here and there among the tall prairie grasses, were green ash trees. Russian thistles rolled across the road that led to the schoolhouse. Heath aster grew wild in our backyard although I was unable to name it. And Mother described the buckbrush at the margin between prairie and the woods along Cub Creek where she grew up.

In 1914, Melvin Gilmore completed his report of interviews with many old Indians of the northern Great Plains. He was particularly interested in showing the close relationship between primitive cultures and their biological surroundings. But in the process of probing their memories, he collected an extensive list of flowering plants of the previous century.

Another source of information regarding life in the near past is the Environmental Impact Statement required before a major project is begun. For example, the construction of levees and floodways to provide flood protection in Mud Creek and the Cottonwood River required a prior study of the area. The study, concluded in 1974, included descriptions of the area's geology, climate, socioeconomic factors, archaeology, history, and plant and animal life. The purpose of these studies is to make governmental agencies and the public aware of the possible side effects of proposed projects. These would include the destruction of an archaeologic site or the destruction of the habitat of an endangered species.

Scholarly studies have also contributed much to our knowledge of the kind of life that existed in the past. Professor John E. Weaver spent 40 summers studying and describing the life of North American grasslands. His studies included the years before, during and after the drought of the 1930s. His work resulted in the first comprehensive book on the subject and was published in 1954.

Shorter-term studies of specific local areas are also useful. Over 300 species of flowering plants were described from Ross Natural History Reservation on the east face of the Flint Hills. Nearly 300 species were collected from Sand Prairie Natural History Reservation in Harvey County. Also identified were 22 species of mammals, 108 of birds, 17 of reptiles, eight of amphibians and four of fish.

Plants described in many of these study areas were collected and preserved in herbarium cases for later reference. The Bethel College herbarium, for example, has specimens of the plant species collected at Sand Prairie. Also in the Bethel College herbarium are 379 plant specimens collected in 1896 by student J.G. Ewert. His Marion County collection included 92 native species, 19 introduced weeds and over a hundred other non-native plants. Ewert became a bedfast cripple but was a prolific writer, a persistent crusader and a gifted professor of nine languages at Tabor College.

Another source of information about life in the past is the notes of naturalists, explorers and travelers. In 1898, J.B. Norton, a graduate student at Kansas Agricultural College, made a two-week trip on foot pushing a wheelbarrow to investigate forage crops in central Kansas. He walked 193 miles from Manhattan across the northwest corner of Marion County on to Rush Center. Norton noted that northern Marion County grasses were chiefly big and little bluestem and switchgrass under good management. Buffalo grass and the gramas were common on hilltops and anywhere pastures were cropped too close.

Diaries are another source of information of past environments. In 1846, on June 25, 18-year-old Susan Magoffin wrote of stopping at Cottonwood Point (near Durham) along the Santa Fe Trail. She described the Cottonwood as a "placid little stream" with a steep bank covered with cottonwood trees. She saw gooseberry and raspberry bushes which had given up most of their fruits to earlier wagoneers.

About 10 days after Susan Magoffin crossed the Cottonwood, there came a contingent of the U.S. Topographical Engineers. Their naturalist, Lieutenant J.W. Abert, wrote extensive descriptions of the plants and animals observed as his party traveled by mule-drawn wagons and horseback from Fort Leavenworth west to Bent's Fort along the Arkansas River in Colorado. Abert recorded daily observations of their surroundings as they passed through or near Council Grove, Diamond Springs, Lost Springs, Cottonwood Fork, Turkey Creek, Pawnee Rock and on. On July 6 to 7 at Cottonwood Fork, he noted the tall cottonwoods with their rustling leaves, thickets of American elder in full bloom, box elder and the wild plums that Susan Magoffin had seen a few days earlier. He observed clear water "in which sported the black bass, the cat fish and the sun fish." Around their camp, the ground was yellow with goldenrods.

So far we have gone back in time only 146 years. Actually we have evidence of the make-up of ecosystems going back millions of years. But that requires a different kind of investigation than the oral or written communication discussed here.

The Healing Prairie

I waded through the knee-high prairie grasses that form a strip between two barbed wire fences separating Marion and Chase counties. The strip marks an abandoned roadway that reaches from Highway K-150 toward the north as far as I can see. Though the roadway was never formally closed, it fell into disuse more than a dozen years ago. The next mile north was formally closed in 1952, according to the county clerk's office.

The former roadway has now healed over, the prairie vegetation having erased any sign of vehicular traffic. Big bluestem, Indian grass, and several finer-leaved mid-grasses dominate. But a rich variety of wildflowers is dispersed among the grasses, and trees and shrubs are scattered along the way, the oldest growing nearest the fences.

It is late afternoon in mid-July and the wild plums are beginning to ripen. Heath asters are abundant but not yet in flower. The buds of prairie goldenrod can hardly contain their yellow treasure. Smooth milkweeds, standing here and there above the grasses, have already lost their blooms. In the prairie, one burst of bloom is followed, shortly, by another burst of other species.

An eastern kingbird makes a brief appearance. Redwings are always in sight. Dickcissels make their busy sounds. Mourning doves are flushed from the shrubs. A ring-necked pheasant catapults from the base of a nearby white mulberry. The sights and sounds here are equally startling.

Fortunately for the birds, there are ripe fruits and seeds ready for harvest; the roasted-brown fruits of curly dock, the waving heads of Canada wild rye, the white shaving brush of wavy-leaf thistle, the bright red hips of the Arkansas rose, the prickly claws of sensitive briar. I have already missed the rose-purple flowers of wild bergamot. And most of the dreamy-lavender blossoms of lead plant have matured.

The shrubs, too, are seeing harvest time. Both smooth and fragrant sumacs offer their deep red, fuzzy "berries." Poison ivy, a close relative of the sumacs, grows in the fence row and twines to the top of a red cedar. A few light-green fruits appear on the dogwood. Fruits are yet to ripen on buckbrush, its colonies reaching from one fence row more than half way to the other.

A wood nymph butterfly flits among the shrubs. At higher altitude, a monarch wings its way along the abandoned roadway.

Also scattered along the fence rows are hackberry and American elm trees performing their roles in the prairie. A brown thrasher flies quietly from one elm to the next. Cowbirds perch momentarily in an elm, keeping one eye on their cattle. Another elm lifts a dead limb skyward and provides a lookout point for a loggerhead shrike. From this perch it can search the ground below for grasshoppers, crickets, and even snakes, lizards and mice. To tear up the larger prey for swallowing, shrikes wedge them into a crotch or impale them on a thorn or the barb of a wire fence.

I admire the occasional white sage scattered among the dark-green grasses, the autumn bouquet of dried yarrow rising from its fine, fern-like leaves, and the very faded blossom of the petunia-like fringed ruellia.

Whorled milkweeds are gathering energy for a bloom later this month or next. Across the fence, some snow-on-the-mountains are about to bloom.

An abrupt break in the terrain: a hip-deep gully, a half meter wide, reaches from a cultivated field of pigweeds and annual sunflowers, across the roadway, into the pasture. The area has seen rain in years past.

A few weedy species have encroached on the roadway from adjacent fields: giant ragweed, Carolina horsenettle and ironweed. But the native vegetation doesn't allow them to dominate.

Close relatives of our State Wildflower abound. Not yet blooming are stiff sunflower and Maximilian sunflower. The tall compass plants are displaying their handsome bouquets. Their large, deeply incised leaves stand erect with their lobes dutifully pointing north and south.

Legumes in this prairie strip noted for returning nitrogen to the soil are sensitive briar, lead plant, and the now-flowering scurfpea. Among the few flowering non-legumes with this capability is the New Jersey tea. Today, it has clusters of tiny saucer-shaped fruit bases which will remain on the plant all winter.

About a mile along the way, three barbed wires stretch across the old roadway. It is toward evening and time to turn back and reflect on what I have seen and heard. The progression of growth, flowering and fruiting continues. If fruiting elicits gratitude for the present, flowering brings hope for the future. The healing of this small piece of prairie from the scars of civilization reflects the toughness of this ecosystem.

I stop to chat briefly with Skip Sieger, a nearby resident. He refers to the drought. His Dempster windmill pumps water for his cattle and his garden. Though his well is 30 meters (150 ft) deep, running all day requires three days for recharge. Neighbors report the drying of some wells and springs for the first time in recent history.

The lushness of the strip of prairie during a year of scant rainfall re-emphasizes the resilience of prairie creatures. This prairie appears to do well in spite of the drought.

Skip has another concern expressed by signs he has placed along the highway: "This highway will be closed if Fort Riley takes this land." That would open the highway and our abandoned roadway to army tank maneuvers. Are there some wounds the prairie cannot heal?

A Boggy Marsh

Nestled in a gentle valley in the Great Bend Prairie of central Kansas is a marsh which comes closer to being a bog than any other I've seen in the Midwest. It was July 1 of 1956 and I walked on a layer of vegetation that floated on the shallow marsh waters like a raft made of flexible carpet. The slight depression left by my departing foot filled quickly with water but each new step was always supported, though waveringly, by the tangle of the roots and stems of the mat-forming grass. Standing tall from the grass mat were occasional swamp milkweeds accompanied by shorter bugleweeds.

The southwestern portion of the marsh abounded with cattails, in which redwings nested, and scattered bulrushes. The eastern end was choked with large-leafed arrowheads which led toward a brook issuing from an iron-cased concrete cylinder. A pipe stood out of the side of the cylinder delivering 23 liters (6 gallons) of clear water per minute. In the brook directing water from the well toward the marsh was a lush growth of watercress. Both the cool water and the tasty watercress refreshed passers-by.

This little oasis between the Big and Little Salt Marshes in Stafford County not only supported my body; it lifted my spirit as well. The sights and sounds of the yellowthroat, the orchard oriole, the eastern meadowlark and the blue grosbeak added to the scene. The experience invited further visits which were made from March in 1957 until August of 1958, and occasional visits since.

Visits to this boggy marsh were inspirational; but they also led to systematic investigations into some of the ecologic relationships in this prairie oasis. Some folks carry a fishing pole or a shotgun to mask their real reasons for tramping into the wilderness; I carried plant presses, chemistry titration units, binoculars and a microscope.

Several questions begged for answers; is the artesian well the only source of water for the marsh? Why such definite zones of vegetation? How does the floating mat of grass develop? Which animals make their home in this marsh?

The artesian well seems to be an obvious source of water. Artesian wells and springs exist where water-bearing strata are capped by clay or rock layers which slope upward away from the point of discharge. Rainfall enters the water-bearing layers where they crop out at higher elevations, and the gravitational force of the water exerts pressure against the confining layers. If a crack develops in or a hole is drilled through the clay or rock cap, water is forced through the rock like water rising through a hole in the bottom of a boat.

Pioneer residents say that this well was drilled by petroleum prospectors in the early 1930s. According to geologists, it is about 12 meters (40 ft) deep and taps water from the sand and gravel of the Meade formation.

Some of the water flows toward the Big Salt Marsh to the north. The rest flows into the boggy marsh where it presumably replenishes the water lost by seepage and evaporation.

Water temperature measurements in the marsh, however, suggest that the well is not the sole source of water in the marsh. Temperature patterns suggested narrow streams of water flowing from the deepest area where cattails surround an open-water area. During a winter visit, marsh waters were capped with ice except in this same open-water area. This, and the looseness of bottom sand during periods of high rainfall, suggested some subsurface recharging of marsh waters. And long-time residents here report that the marsh existed before the well was drilled.

●　　●　　●

The boggy marsh set in the lowland prairie of central Kansas had definite vegetation zones. Arrowheads congregated in the narrow channel between the artesian well and the marsh. Surrounding the deepest open water area were the cattails. Tiny duckweeds floated in the open water zone. And the broad floating mat north of the cattails was composed of the tangled mass of the roots and stems of rice cutgrass.

Zonation of plants was probably not due to differences in water chemistry. After all, the water was coming from only two sources; the deeper artesian well and near-surface water table. More likely, it was the different plant communities with associated water and mud creatures that modified the water chemistry.

So, what caused the zonation?

To answer that question, I first documented the population density of the various species of dominant plants. In organized fashion, I stretched binder twine across the marsh and counted the number of times any plant parts of each species intercepted the space beneath each meter of twine. Ten parallel transects covered the marsh. I stood in the marsh in hip boots and with a tally register in hand, identifying, counting and announcing the names and numbers to Elaine who was on the bank of the marsh recording data. Likewise, we measured water depth and both thickness and compactness of bottom mud in each zone.

We noted that the rice cutgrass was most abundant in the moist solid soil where excess marsh waters flowed over into nearby grasslands. Perhaps there was a succession of plant communities, the sequence of species determined by their ability to survive in and further solidify the bottom mud.

Lakes and ponds tend to fill with silt through time. This filling in affects the kinds of plants found in each zone of the pond. Aquatic plants give way to marsh plants which are replaced by land plants until only land plants survive. In this marsh, though, little silt was washed in from the surrounding grassland. We sought a different reason for ecologic succession.

In this marsh, emerging cattails surrounded the deepest open water zone. Cattails germinate best in moisture, in light and where oxygen concentration is low. Since oxygen is not very soluble in water, the mud at the bottom of this clear water is an ideal seedbed for cattails. As the cattail rhizomes multiply and then die, they enrich the mud and their roots begin to consolidate the soil. If rainfall is fairly low and an upwelling of groundwater does not occur, the consolidating mud allows seedlings of water parsnip and bur marigold to mature. Their ability to root at the joints of their stems further provides reinforcement for bottom mud. Finally, rice cutgrass can survive and flourish.

The floating aspect of the mat seemed more pronounced after periods of heavier rainfall, when upwelling of waters into the marsh occurred. Perhaps this water pressure from below the grass mat lifted it slightly above the sand layer.

This sequence of events seemed to provide a logical explanation for the boggy conditions in the marsh.

While I concluded that "water chemistry had no apparent effect on the distribution of aquatic seed plants," this may not be true of all organisms here. Certain species are most commonly found in the well-oxygenated, cool headwaters of artesian or spring brooks. Watercress is one such plant. So is the yellow-green, filamentous alga, *Vaucheria*, found here near the well.

Two species of animals also found their preferred habitat here. *Attheyella nordenskioldii*, an almost microscopic crustacean, was not found elsewhere in the marsh. Indeed, this was the only reported observation of this species in Kansas.

The brown planaria, a free-living relative of tapeworms, was usually observed near the well outlet. This species of flatworm is known for its ability to regenerate missing body parts, its avoidance of light and its tendency to swim against current, keeping it in fresh headwaters of streams.

Microscopic observations of this worm's large, "friendly" crossed eyes made up for the threats we experienced in this boggy marsh from a massasauga rattlesnake, the tales of livestock disappearing in the quicksand of the marsh and the looks of local folks who probably suspected that we were involved with the move to make this marsh part of the then-proposed Quivira National Wildlife Refuge.

The Gypsum Creek Nature Trail

Near the observation tower at Maxwell Game Refuge, several American bison graze peacefully in the bluestem grassland. Only a tough wire fence separates us from their massive brown bodies. One bull performs his clumsy dust-rolling ritual before our very eyes. Skyward, toward the lake, a turkey vulture glides on air currents, oblivious to our excitement over the bison.

On July 18, daughter Kris and grandchildren Ashley, 8, and Andrew, 4, stopped here with me to explore the refuge. Satisfied with our views of bison, we round the McPherson County State Lake to hike the nature trail on the east-facing slope southwest of the lake.

From an upland clearing, the trail descends quickly to the wooded edges of Gypsum Creek. It then ascends to the uplands, possibly of sand dune origin, and back down again to a pool in the creek.

The trail was prepared in 1983 and was originally accompanied by a guide booklet. Some described features have changed in nine years. But we have learned to expect change; erosion/deposition, living/dying, growing/decaying, eating/being eaten.

The first marked point of interest is a soil profile display prepared by the McPherson County Soil Conservation District. It relates the soil to the geology of the area.

The surrounding woods is a mix of hackberry, mulberry, osage orange, black walnut, catalpa, and other hardwood trees.

The trail disappears into the trees. On the damp ground are white avens with small green fruits, and chervil with tiny white flowers and fernlike leaves.

On the upward slope, away from the trees, are blooming American elders with their huge flower clusters and the blue flowers of spiderwort and dayflower. Also in bloom are horsemint with its aromatic leaves, pokeberry already with a few immature fruits, the tiny yellow wood sorrel, and a yellow evening primrose. Clusters of smooth sumac, rough-leaved dogwood, and buckbrush consolidate the soil on the sandy slope.

Back among the trees, tall vines of wild grape and poison ivy climb tree trunks, reaching for light.

A poison ivy vine close to a box elder tree provides an opportunity to point out the similarities and differences in their compound leaves. The leaf of each species is composed of three stalked leaflets that are coarsely toothed. (Box elder may have as many as seven leaflets per leaf.) The ivy leaves are arranged singly on alternate sides of the stem. The box elder's leaves are arranged in pairs, on opposite sides of the stem.

But today it is easiest to recognize the difference by their fruits. A poison ivy fruit is creamy white and shaped like a tiny pumpkin the size of a small pea. Each box elder fruit is straw-colored when ripe and has a large wing extending from a flattened seed. (It is a maple.) To those folks who develop an allergy to poison ivy, it is important to know the difference.

On the sandy uplands is another variety of blooms; the large white bowl of prickly poppy, the bleached blue of Carolina horse-nettle, the deep cherry-red of purple poppymallow, and the light blue ruellia. Past the bloom stage and now fruiting are yarrow, trailing wild bean, and both sand milkweed and Sullivant milkweed with their spindle-shaped pods. Between aromatic sumac shrubs are white-leaved white sage. Sandhill plums are in fruit, most not fully ripe. Escaping our wandering feet is a quickly disappearing lizard. He makes his home here among the prickly pear cactus and the yucca.

The sound of an energetic house wren comes from the woods below. A throaty yellow-billed cuckoo sings. We hear redwings down on the cattails in the creek. A bullfrog splashes into the stream and disturbs the arrangement of free floating duckweeds. A kingfisher screams at a distance. Ten-spot dragonflies patrol the pool, no doubt searching for insects which they eat on the wing. We also see the delicate damselflies which, like dragonflies, lay their eggs in or on water plants, or directly in the water.

Near the end of the return trail, the kids are tired and hungry. Drew wants me to carry him up the last hill. We find a place to eat our packed lunch and enjoy the relaxing scene the prairie hillside offers.

Mulberries and Silkworms

If it weren't for silkworms, we might not have white mulberries on these prairies. Let me explain.

There are two species of mulberry in the Midwest. The native red mulberry, *Morus rubra*, grows to a height of 18 meters and grows on the rich flood plains and creek banks of the eastern three-fifths of Kansas. Its leaves are usually 10 to 18 cm long and hairy beneath.

The introduced white mulberry, *Morus alba*, is usually limited to low crowns eight meters high and grows in the open prairie throughout the state. Its leaves are only six to ten centimeters long and usually lack hairs beneath or have only a few hairs on its veins. Its leaves are variously lobed. Its multiple fruits are either white, purple or black.

The white mulberry originated in China but was planted in colonial Virginia as early as 1623. Various introductions have resulted in its widespread use as a shade tree and as a component of shelterbelts across the United States. The male tree, being fruitless, is used where fallen fruits would stain sidewalks below or attract flies. Some individuals bear both male and female flowers.

The white mulberry was introduced to Europe and America primarily to promote the silk industry. Early American settlers, including George Washington and Benjamin Franklin, planted them as food for silkworms.

In Kansas, silk production began in the 1870s when silkworms and a variety of white mulberry were introduced by the Russian Mennonites. They had practiced silk production on a small scale in the Ukraine.

Commercial silk is produced by the larvae (silkworms) of *Bombyx mori*, a white moth with black-lined wings that span about five centimeters. The female moth lays 300 to 500 eggs which hatch into larvae in about 20 days. Each green larva feeds voraciously on newly wilted white mulberry leaves almost continuously for four or five weeks until the silkworm is about seven centimeters long. Then it stops eating and begins forming its cocoon. The silk that forms the cocoon originates from the milky sap of the white mulberry and is secreted by two glands near the silkworm's lower jaw. The secretion hardens as soon as it contacts the air. The two strands are cemented together with a gum called sericin. After three days of wrapping the silk around itself, the larva becomes a pupa. The pupa matures in about three weeks and bursts from its cocoon by cutting the one double strand into many pieces. To prevent this destruction, the silk is harvested by killing the pupa, usually with heat. Then the double strands are unwound and combined with others to form a thread.

In 1882, an observer visited several Marion County farms where silkworms were cultured and cocoons were processed. He noted that "the work required infinite patience, of which few Americans are possessed."

By 1885, there was enough interest in silk production to warrant the formation of the Kansas Silk Association. Two years later, the Kansas Legislature appropriated $13,000 to establish a silk station just north of Peabody. There, cocoons were processed and mulberry leaves were stored. S.L. Loewen, retired Tabor College biology teacher, recalls that his father planted mulberry trees on the 10-acre site of the Peabody station. An additional silk station was organized at Hillsboro.

But the cold, rainy weather of those years, the labor required and cheap foreign silk made sericulture unprofitable in Kansas. The Peabody silk station was closed in 1897. All that remains is fence rows of white mulberry trees, probably descendants of those that fed silkworms a century ago and a few cocoons and masses of reeled silk on display at the Peabody Historical Museum. Similar fate awaited sericulture throughout the United States.

Though silk culture was short-lived here, other uses of the introduced mulberry continued. S.L. Loewen recalls putting the fruits into a tub of water and, with brothers and sisters, tramping on them barefooted to separate seeds from the pulp. The William Schaeffler store in Hillsboro paid them about 75 cents per pound of cleaned seeds.

What Good Is It?

"What good is it?" He pointed to a plant anchored in the sandy soil of the South

Ninnescah valley in Kingman County. Competing with prairie grasses for space, light, water and soil minerals, this plant had valiantly assembled the biochemical apparatus with which it converts water and carbon dioxide into complex carbohydrates. The plant converts some of these carbohydrates into proteins, oils and a few special compounds unique to its family.

The human body is capable of miraculous chemical feats, but it cannot begin to accomplish what this green plant does routinely. Our bodies just can't manufacture food from simple inorganic substances.

In addition to these chemical miracles, this prairie jewel "knows" how to reproduce itself so that like-plants can appear next season even if this one doesn't survive the long, dry winter.

I wonder what prompted the "What good is it?" I grew up among prairie creatures, wondering who they were, and thrilled by their sounds, their fragrances, their varied textures, their colors, their shapes, their fascinating habits and their complex interactions. But I don't recall questioning their value. I certainly didn't presume that the bewildering variety of organisms was designed specifically to satisfy my needs and whims.

When Benjamin Franklin tinkered with the curious behavior of electrons, someone asked him, "What good is electricity?" He replied, "What good is a baby?"

Perhaps it is part of the human condition to look at the world from the vantage point of self. In this materialistic culture, we are programmed to judge things, and even people, from the standpoint of what personal advantage we can wrench from them. Personal commitment to great causes appears to be eroding. Is it possible that this basic selfishness, this greed, coupled with ignorance of the world around us, is responsible for the environmental crises facing this prairie and our whole planet today? The pioneer attitude that the world is out there for us to exploit may gratify our fantasies, but it is devastating our home planet.

We need to see the biosphere as an intricately integrated system in which each species— poison ivy, rattlesnakes and tapeworms included—plays a vital role in the wholeness of the ecosystem of which it is a part. This is true in forests, marshes, deserts and coral reefs as well as prairies. Once we understand the importance of the wholeness of ecosystems, we see that we need to find our own place in this grand scheme, not as exploiters, but as fellow creatures interdependent with all living things.

The principle of enlightened self-interest suggests that ultimately, I will survive only if I cooperate with the natural world. Social Security, savings accounts, stocks and bonds, the military establishment—all are meaningless if we destroy our air, water and soil.

When friends of prairie ecologist David Costello point to a creature and ask, "What good is it?" he responds: "It is good in that it plays a part in the web of life...the mere presence of anything, living or nonliving, seems to be sufficient justification for its existence."

The mere existence of that plant in the sandy prairie indicates that it has served, and continues to serve, some function in that great web of which I, too, am a small part.

Walking On Water

The box canyon at Elm Springs is filled with the lush growth of various deciduous trees, choke cherries, bittersweet, poison ivy and blackberry bushes. On this July forenoon, a garden-hose-size stream of spring water drops into the canyon from the rock ledge above. The shaded plunge pool below is patrolled by black winged damselflies with iridescent green bodies. And on the surface of the shaded pool, water striders are skating this way and that as they have for at least 30 million years. This appears to be *Gerris remigis*, the most common species in Kansas and much of North America.

Simple principles of physics explain the striders' ability to walk on water. For one, they exploit the surface tension of water. Surface tension is what forms the "skin" over the surface of water that can hold up a needle. Water molecules attract each other. Those at the upper surface are pulled together and down, requiring some force for an object to pry those surface molecules apart.

One biologist calculated that a sheep, a million times as heavy as a water strider, would need feet with a total length of seven kilometers (4.3 miles) to support its weight by surface tension. Walking on water, he concluded, is feasible only for small animals. The largest of strider species in Kansas is only 15 mm long.

An aid to surface tension is the coat of non-wetting hairs on the feet that rest on the water.

Water striders may also take advantage of water's buoyancy. Any object submerged in or floating on a fluid is buoyed up by a force equal to the weight of the displaced fluid. A boat floats because it is shaped to displace more than its own weight of water. As long as a strider's legs do not break the water's surface, the deeper the dent into the surface, the more the upward buoyant force.

Surface tension, water-repelling hairs, and buoyancy keep a water strider from breaking the water surface all but three times in its 30-to-45-day life span. Only after it hatches underwater, and as a female dips her abdomen to deposit eggs underwater and as a dying adult loses its water-repelling properties, does a water strider break the water surface.

But what do these striders do on the water? Mostly, they wait for other insects to fall on the water and provide a meal, or they wait for maturing insects, such as mosquitoes, to leave their water nursery for adult life in the air.

The strider's mouthparts are long and pointed and can pierce the tough outer skeleton of most insects. Holding its prey with its front legs, it injects enzymes that liquify the prey's insides. The strider then sucks out body fluids and discards the empty exoskeleton.

To locate their prey, striders use both their sharp vision and the wave receptors in their legs. The wave receptors are also used in mating communication. In one species, the male anchors himself with his front legs and generates ripples in the water with his hind and middle legs. These ripples are intended to attract mates and, possibly, to establish territory.

Among the predators of adult striders are other insects, fish and ducks. Quick jumps powered by both hind legs help avoid being captured.

But nothing the striders can do protects them from human destruction of their habitat. And water pollution often lowers surface tension and causes striders to sink and drown. Our modern lifestyles are among the greatest threats to the existence of the water strider, another creature in this great web of life.

Pipestone Creek

Lowell Goering and I followed the trail along Pipestone Creek in southwest Minnesota. To the north lay virgin upland prairie displaying July blossoms of common prairie species. On the south, along the course of the creek, is the small pond called Lake Hiawatha. Forest and forest-edge species are prominent along the stream. At several locations along the trail are quarry pits from which the Dakota Sioux and other tribes of Plains Indians have dug pipestone for the past several centuries.

Pipestone is a durable but relatively soft stone ranging in color from mottled pink to brick-red. It is prized by Indians for its attractive appearance and its carveability. Many tribes used it for making the ceremonial pipes used in rituals related to warfare, peace, trading, dancing and medicine. The stone and the pipes were objects of trade, reaching out into the plains.

Attached to the carved T-shaped bowl was a long stem of ash or other hardwood. The stem was split lengthwise and the central pith scraped from both halves which were rejoined with sap glue and cord. Color and decoration of stems varied with tribe and function. Present-day Indians use twigs of smooth sumac and hot wire to burn out its core in forming the hollow pipestem.

Only Native Americans are allowed to dig pipestone from these pits. The area was considered as sacred ground by some quarriers and only men were allowed to enter the quarries. All tribes recognized this area as a peace shrine where ancient enmities were forgotten.

The distant sound of a waterfall increases as the trail approaches the prominent ledge of Sioux quartzite running north and south across Pipestone Creek. Creek waters at Winnewissa

Falls descend the ledge and flow on toward Lake Hiawatha.

In the early 1900s, the falls were lowered by nearly three meters by blasting the rim to create additional tillable land. This changed the course of Pipestone Creek and contaminated its waters with silt, a continuing problem.

The pipestone here underlies the Sioux quartzite. Geologists speculate that this area was submerged in coastal sea waters eons ago. The pipestone originated as a deposit of muddy clay which became covered with a deep layer of sand.

Of great personal interest to me is the identical composition of these huge deposits of Sioux quartzite and the boulders and rocks my mother helped clear from her parents' farm 420 km (260 miles) to the south in southeast Nebraska. Could it be that the red and purple rocks on that Nebraska farm, and others in northeast Kansas, originated along Pipestone Creek in Minnesota? Indeed, it is very likely that they came from Pipestone, or deposits in nearby areas, bulldozed by glaciers that plowed southward into Kansas several hundred thousand years ago.

A Hollow Cottonwood

A hollow tree generates cautious curiosity. I wouldn't want to miss an adventure with a raccoon or a cottontail. But neither would I want to corner a skunk or a rattlesnake.

The hollow trunk of this eastern cottonwood stands firmly in the bottomland along the South Ninnescah River. I have passed it often, but this time I ponder its niche in the prairie community.

Although most of its heartwood has decayed, this cottonwood is very much alive, displaying its glistening triangular leaves to the Kansas sun. And they are carrying on their proper food-making function. Some of their food is directed through the trunk, by tiny tubes just inside its outer bark, to its hungry roots.

The tissues that conduct water and dissolved minerals from the soil to the leaves make up the bulk of the trunk. Most of these inner tissues have by now become filled with dried sap and no longer allow the flow of liquids. So the plugged up heartwood can rot away without disturbing the day-to-day functions of the trunk, as long as enough "open" wood remains just inside the bark.

This hollow tree is available to animals as protection from severe weather and hungry predators, or as a place to raise their young. So one might see tracks of opossums, raccoons, eastern cottontails, bobcats or striped skunks leading to and from the entrance.

The limbs of this grand cottonwood might serve as a roosting place for bats and great horned owls, or the blue jays that scream at them. These limbs provide nesting sites for fox squirrels and woodpeckers. Across nearby Sand Creek, red-headed woodpeckers have, with persistent pecking, carved out holes in dead cottonwoods in which they lay their white eggs on the wood chips that line the bottom.

Other nearby cottonwoods have been harvested by beaver. Their tooth marks are still visible on pointed stumps. Beaver gnaw off cottonwoods for winter food or, in forested areas, for building lodges or dams. They have felled trees up to 1.5 meters in diameter.

Beaver feed eagerly on the buds, inner bark and leaves of the cottonwood. To a lesser degree, eastern cottontails, fox squirrels, and white-tailed deer feed on the same tissues.

The Plains Indians ate the peeled cottonwood sprouts and inner bark for their taste and nutritional value. They fed young branches to their horses.

But probably as important to the Indians as these common uses were the mystic properties attributed to the cottonwood. The Sacred Pole of the Omaha Indians was made of cottonwood. It fulfilled a function similar to that of the Ark of the Covenant for the ancient Hebrews.

Melvin Gilmore, early in this century, interviewed many Plains Indians gathering information regarding their old ways. He suggested that their respect for the cottonwood related to its self-reliance, its great reproductive capacity, its lustrous foliage and its restless leaves. It is found not only along streams, but also out in the open plains. Even a fresh green twig thrust into moist ground grows to maturity. And its leaves never rest, "reflecting the splendor of the sun like the dancing ripples of a lake."

I have spent the night alone nearly under this cottonwood and, during waking moments, listened to the night sounds. Even with no detectable breeze, I could hear the gentle rustling of its leaves. A look at the leaf stalk reveals the secret; its flattened shape allows even a tiny breeze to wiggle the leaf. Gilmore says that, to the Indians, the winds "were the paths of the Higher Powers, so they were constantly reminded of the mystical character of this tree."

But the sacred attributes of the cottonwood did not prevent Indian children from using it in their play. They joined the sloping margins of a leaf, fastening them with a thorn to make a tepee. Leaves and thorns were also used to make moccasins.

Girls and young women made pleasing sounds with the cottonwood leaf. Forcing their breath past a leaf's edge produced a vibration which created sweet flute-like notes.

Indians used the root wood of cottonwood to start fires by friction. Indians and early European settlers alike used the wood for campfires as it burns quickly and leaves few coals.

But this cottonwood isn't ready to become fuel. It has food to make, nests to hold, shade to cast and secrets to whisper. And it has shelter to provide in its hollow trunk.

Reading the Rocks

Under an overcast August sky, the land northeast of Florence looks like an African savanna before a rare shower. Shrubby elms and red cedars are scattered among the grasses and forbs in this upland prairie. Senescent heads of Canada wild rye and blooming stalks of big bluestem are reaching high above the blue grama grass. Also among the grasses are purple bouquets of ironweed, white-capped snow-on-the-mountain, a few huddled stalks of willow-leaved sunflower, soft-violet blossoms of lead plant and the light olive leaves of both Texas and wooly crotons. One last pink ball of a sensitive briar remains. The persistent dark globes of matured purple coneflowers stand above the short grasses.

Then the floor of the prairie drops abruptly into a 10-meter-deep, flat-bottomed chasm larger than a football field. Its vertical edges expose the gray-white strata of Fort Riley and Florence Limestones often separated by a thin layer of Oketo Shale. These rocks have been blasted loose, crushed and transported to roads and construction sites. Piles of crushed rock are being formed now on the west bank of the quarry by the Florence Rock Company.

As interesting as the present use of the rock, is its origin. By studying the chemical composition and the embedded fossils of rock outcroppings, geologists correlate strata that crop out in various locations. For example, Fort Riley Limestone is recognized by certain characteristics and is always found above Florence Limestone which has its own unique features. As in this quarry, Florence Limestone often includes scattered nodules of chert, also called flint.

Geologists do not fully understand the origin of chert. Some think that Kansas chert resulted from the presence of sponges, primitive animals in ancient seas. The sponges formed spicules of silica which they extracted from sea water. Somehow, the silica coalesced to form chert.

Embedded in this quarry exposure is the fossilized lace bryozoan *Fenestrellina*, a net-veined, fan-shaped sea creature. Also imprisoned in this limestone for several hundred million years is a fossilized brachiopod (probably *Squamaria*) which resembles a walnut-size clam. Apparently, this creature died on the sea floor and was covered with sediment. The entombed brachiopod shell dissolved away and the resulting cavity was filled with limestone to form this cast. Bryozoan species existing today are most abundant in shallow marine seas.

In addition to outcroppings and quarry activity, core drillings provide direct evidence of the mineral composition and the kinds of fossils present in the various strata deep in Earth's crust. Geologists have available for study more than 130,000 oil drillers' logs, 35,000 electric and radioactivity logs and 10,000 sample logs for Kansas alone. By now, we have a pretty good picture of the arrangement of rock layers under our feet, and of the ecosystems that produced them.

Rock strata exposed at the surface of this county are of Permian age deposited at the bottom of shallow seas 230 to 280 million years ago. Younger deposits have eroded away. And wherever agriculture is practiced, this erosion continues at a quickening pace. Where less soluble rocks like chert occur, erosion is resisted and hills remain, while nearby valleys are cut more deeply. The Flint Hills display this kind of differential erosion.

In a geologic time frame, this erosion of crustal material is offset by the periodic encroachment of sea waters. Ocean sedimentation again builds up rock strata on the eroded surface of previous layers. These new strata, at some later geologic period, will again be exposed and subject to erosion.

This repeated cycle of sedimentation and erosion is evidenced by the arrangement of layers in Earth's crust. Usually, the coarser sediment is deposited nearer to its source. Gravel and sands are generally dropped nearer to shore in shallow waters where agitation of the delivering stream is no longer sufficient to keep them in suspension. Shales usually indicate deeper waters because fine clay remains in suspension longer as continental waters flow out to sea. Inorganic limestone deposits occur in deeper waters. A layer of inorganic limestone directly above shale or shale above sandstone generally suggests deposits of an advancing sea. Strata arranged in reversed order suggest a receding sea.

Reading the rocks can help give us a picture of the geologic conditions that existed during various time periods at a specific place.

Meanwhile, recent dirt slides at the south edge of the quarry are held in place by the roots of common ragweeds, blooming buffalo bur and the petunia-like ruellia. Pitcher's sage is displaying its blue blossoms to visiting bees. Clouded sulphur and monarch butterflies flit from flower to flower as a clumsy bumblebee stumbles around in the head of a sunflower. A turkey vulture glides high overhead and several killdeer sound their insistent *kill-deeah* as they take off from the quarry floor. Up, on the quarry rim, hoofprints of deer betray their recent presence.

I ponder for a moment the belief that the "laws of nature" are independent of the passage of time, that the fundamental characteristics of the universe, the interactions of matter and energy, remain constant. Isn't there something grand and reassuring about that?

Fossil Pollen From Kansas Swamps

The hot summer sun baked the creek bed where Jack and I were digging out shaley layers from the creek's bank. If there was only one place in the Midwest unlikely to allow a breeze this summer, surely it was here.

The dry creek curves among the undulating Flint Hills uplands in the Neosho River Watershed about five miles west of Americus. Down the slope from a surface outcropping of Cottonwood Limestone, the creek has eroded into the Eskridge Shale.

These strata of gray or tan limey shales contain imprints and even carbon remains of leaves of plants now long extinct. Fossil spores and pollen grains extracted here provide further evidence of a very different scene here 250 million years ago.

Supported by a grant from the National Science Foundation, Jack Sensintaffer and I spent the summer of 1959 unearthing and analyzing evidence of an ecosystem now long past. Paleobotanist Gilbert Leisman supervised the study.

A shaley layer about a half meter thick appeared to be the most productive. Of this, the upper portions revealed carbonized fossil material and occasional coaly layers two millimeters thick. The lower tan shales were even more productive, containing distinct imprints of seed fern leaves. (Seed ferns had fern-like leaves but, unlike ferns, produced seeds.) Underlying these productive strata were two to three centimeters of fossil-bearing limestone.

The shale here was soft, often moist, and easily removed with a putty knife or shovel. Both compression and impression fossils were exposed. Compressions are actual remains of organisms from which high temperatures and pressures have forced out all substance except carbon. Impressions are the imprints of fossil remains in the entombing sediment. When the burying sediments were converted into shale, the enclosed carbonized plant formed a plane of weakness. Upon removal from their deposit, fractures expose the carbonized fossils like opening a book reveals its contents.

Laboratory identification of fossil leaves was based largely on shape, vein patterns, and mode of attachment of leaf units. Without access to authentic specimens for comparison, we relied heavily on excellent photographs, drawings, and written descriptions by authorities in Kansas, Missouri, Pennsylvania, and Illinois.

Preparation of spores and pollen grains was more difficult for they needed to be prepared for higher power microscopic observation. Ridding the quarter-thimble quantity of shale dust of its mineral sediments required treatment with hydrochloric and hydrofluoric acids. These acids dissolved the mineral sediments that interfere with microscope observation. They do this without attacking the outer coats of pollen grains and spores. In every step of this involved process, care was required to prevent contamination by modern spores or pollen grains suspended in the air of the field or laboratory.

As with the fossil leaves, the microfossils were identified from detailed microphotographs, drawings, and written descriptions. Much help came from German and Russian literature.

Of the species of compression/impression fossils found here in Lyon County, one was also collected by others in Pottawatomie County; another in Washington County; and a third in the Appalachian region. A paleontologist passing through Kansas found among our specimens numerous species that he encountered in corresponding strata in Texas. Many of our microfossils corresponded with those in Europe and Russia as well. This is not surprising since Earth's single continent didn't break up into today's separate continents until about this time in geologic history.

The strata observed in Lyon County and the strata generally cropping out in the Flint Hills are from the Lower (older) Permian time. The traces of coal and the profusion of fossil fern and seed fern leaves, spores, and pollen grains support the view that this part of Kansas' surface was once covered with large swamps and marshes. The even more productive coal-bearing strata below these layers cropping out in eastern Kansas indicate that these swamp conditions were even more widespread in still earlier times.

Layers of limestone and shale above and below our study layer suggest that shallow seas came and went numerous times during Permian time, and that marshes and swamps were relatively short episodes during Permian time. But these marshes did support the plants that, though now extinct, were the ancestors of plants that we see today in our forests and prairies, and that meet our everyday needs for nutrition, medicine, shelter, and beauty.

Hiking the Smoky Hills

Traveling through the farmland of northern Marion County toward Carlton, there appears a sudden panoramic view of the Smoky Hills. While most of the county's surface is of Permian age, here in the northwest the younger 100-million-year-old Cretaceous formations have not yet eroded from atop the Permian rocks. These clays and sandstones form rounded hills clothed with prairie grasses and wildflowers under an August sky accented by billowy white clouds. Named for the hazy appearance of their valleys, the Smoky Hills rival the Flint Hills in their beauty.

I cross the barbed-wire fence carefully (to protect my pants as well as the integrity of the fence). Among the flowering big bluestems are clumps of sideoats grama with their separate florets all along one side of the flowering stalk. Many ironweeds have passed their brilliant purple stage and goldenrods are just beginning their splashes of yellow. This year's rains have been good to snow-on-the-mountains. The beauty of their upper white leaves against the lush prairie grasses rivals that of the clouds against the sky.

I am interrupted briefly by the sight of a weathered board apparently ripped from a building, nails protruding upward. It seems out of place here. I turn it over to avoid someone's stepping on the nail. Or am I the only one to wander in the Smoky Hills?

To mount the next hill for a survey of the countryside, I must first descend to the pond and cross the earthen dam.

Recent rains have filled the pond and the overflow area is still a mud flat with numerous small puddles. While crossing the flat, I catch a brief glimpse of the snout of a catfish in a tiny pool. Unless we get a significant rain soon, that fish is doomed in its small prison. I reach into the muddied waters to transport it back to the pond.

Surprise! The snout of a "catfish" turns out to be one edge of the shell of a western painted turtle about the size of my outstretched hand. After a night underwater, this turtle has spent its day basking and feeding. It consumes both plant and animal matter, dead or alive. It obviously doesn't need my assistance. I apologize for the disturbance.

Up the slope, I notice more late summer bloomers. Hoary vervain displays its dense spikes of blue flowers. I spot occasional blue asters and scurfpeas. Blooms of the petunia-like ruellia are common. Near the upper slopes, blue sage is in full bloom, attracting bees to administer cross-pollination.

I note a single rock twice the size of my fist among the grasses. It is sandstone. From the summit, binoculars reveal bluffs of what appears to be sandstone in the hills further north.

Closer in, blue grama grass is in bloom, florets crowded along a stalk to form a flag. Here and there, lead plants are blooming and harboring nitrogen-fixing bacteria to sustain the richness of prairie soils here in the Smoky Hills.

●   ●   ●

The tattered fence divides Marion County from its northern neighbor, Dickinson County. The prairie here is an eastward intrusion of the Smoky Hills into these counties. Since cattle occupy the north area, I choose to explore the south pasture.

The density of ironweed, buffalo bur, ragweed and mat spurge suggest that cattle have long over-grazed or trampled this corner of the grassland. A livestock loading chute and a pasture gate suggest some reasons for this trampling.

I head straight east through a shallow, mostly dry stream bed and on into more balanced prairie. Meadowlarks are no longer singing their mating songs. Now, some fly silently away as I approach. Others perch on a fence or a red cedar and protest my presence. They may be incubating eggs or rearing their fledglings in grassy nests on the prairie floor.

Several stretches of fence along the way are twisted and battered to the ground. Even trees that had grown in the fencerow were severely damaged or even uprooted. While no buildings are in sight, chunks of corrugated metal rest on the sandy soil. I am reminded of the weathered board so out of place on the hillside seen earlier. Tornadic winds have visited this prairie.

I follow the sandy cattle path that roughly parallels the fence. Several fecal droppings indicate that a deer has followed a similar route before me.

The deep cherry-red of purple poppymallow flowers calls attention to their place among other prairie plants. Mourning doves fly over the snakecotton with its wooly white flowers.

Whirring wings carry two quail across the battered fence to escape my threatening camera.

I see occasional camphor weeds and remember the odor of their crushed leaves. Some Indians drank a concoction from camphor weed leaves and stems as a soothing aid to sleep. I thought of the menthol camphor ointment my mother bought from the Watkins man that visited our home periodically. I admire the soft olive green leaves of Texas croton. Nearby is a thicket of chickasaw plum, its fruit long gone. This shrub provides cover for a variety of birds and mammals.

Another artifact, a piece of an old rusty handsaw. Most of its blade is missing as is much of its wooden handle. How did it get here?

A lone prickly pear cactus stands low in the sandy soil.

And the boulder! Protruding from among the grasses is a sandstone rock about a meter high and occupying about one square meter at its base. It has the rusty-brown color of the Dakota sandstone that composes the boulders and bluffs of the Smoky Hills. It shows the scars of weathering by winds, hail, sleet, rain and solar heat. Geologists say that these boulders and bluffs are the remains of old off-shore bars and ancient stream channels which crossed the muds and silts of central Kansas during Cretaceous times. I'll hike closer to the bluffs another time. Meanwhile, I notice the tall gayfeather with buttons of purple flowers along its stalk.

Common St. John's-wort is still blooming. But I never see its populations threatening the grasslands in the great plains. Further west, this introduced species has become troublesome and is known as klamathweed. A poison found in its foliage causes photosensitization in livestock that eat it. It becomes active when light-skinned animals are exposed to light.

Returning to my starting point, I cross the dry, shallow streambed toward the pasture gate. The nodding stalk of velvety gaura waves goodbye in a gentle breeze. A young eastern cottontail scampers across the fence into the next county. Someday, I'll accept its invitation to hike further into the Smoky Hills.

Cross-Pollination in Pitcher Sage

Pitcher sage is a remarkable plant found on rocky or sandy hillsides and uplands in Missouri and southern Nebraska, across Kansas and Oklahoma, into Texas. Its sky-blue flower not only produces nectar but it provides a landing platform to accommodate nectar-collecting insects.

Even more remarkable are additional mechanisms in Pitcher sage that relate to cross-pollination. Cross-pollination is important in many species because it increases variation of inherited characteristics in offspring. If a significant climatic or geologic change occurs, it is more likely that some of a variety of offspring would have the combination of traits appropriate for survival in the changed environment. With no variation, either all or none would survive successfully.

Male flower deposits pollen on bee's back and older female flower receives it.

In Pitcher sage, several characteristics combine to insure cross-pollination. One is the difference in time of maturity of the male and female parts of the flower. If within a certain flower, the pollen is ripe before or after the female part is ripe, self-pollination cannot occur.

In Pitcher sage, the male part of the flower

ripens first. Rotating lever-like around a short stalk is the pollen bearing anther. The nectar-seeking bee pushes the low short end of the anther forward and upward. Therefore the upper, longer, pollen-bearing end swings down and deposits its pollen on the top of the bee's abdomen.

In older flowers, pollen is no longer present and the female style has lengthened and matured, ready to receive pollen. It now touches the back of any visiting bee and receives ripe pollen from the younger flowers the bee recently visited.

But this elaborate mechanism is inoperative if the bee can't see the flowers. That's where the blue flower color comes in. While humans can distinguish about 60 distinct colors, bees see only four; yellow, blue-green, blue and ultra-violet. If the flowers of Pitcher sage were red, they would look black to a bee.

It appears that flowers are adapted to the color sense of their visitors, not for the delight of human admirers. There is something magnificent about seeing more in the grand scheme of the prairie than just pretty flowers.

A member of the mint family, Pitcher sage is a perennial with square stems about one meter tall. In Kansas, it is found primarily in the east three-fourths of the state. Its many flowers are clustered in terminal spikes.

The common name refers to Dr. Z. Pitcher, a surgeon and botanist. The official name, *Salvia azurea*, is from the Latin "*salvare*," to heal, as some species have medicinal uses; and *azurea* refers to its flower color, which delights the eye of the botanist and the occasional prairie wanderer alike.

The Snow-on-the-Mountain

It was late August of 1976 along Kansas Highway 15, just north of the road leading to the old Hollenberg Pony Express Station in Washington County. Out in the pasture, paralleling the highway, was a distinct two-meter-wide strip of snow-on-the-mountain plants. This handsome native of the Midwest is often cultivated as an ornamental. But this was an overgrazed pasture!

Evidence of recent soil disruption and the tall tank of a rural water district over the next hill suggested the burial of a water line. Found occasionally in limestone soils of undisturbed prairies, snow-on-the-mountain quickly expands into overgrazed pastures, flood plains, roadsides and abandoned cultivated fields. The water pipe was probably buried the previous summer or fall and seeds from nearby areas were dispersed over the bare soil for full growth by this August.

While the flowers are white, most of the whiteness of this spurge is due to the white margins of the upper leaves, especially those immediately under the flowers. Even the latex that oozes from wounds in the plant is white, often causing observers to mistake the plant for milkweed.

The milky latex contains the little-understood poison, euphorbon. The latex causes skin inflammation in many persons. Even honey made from its nectar is reported to be poisonous to human consumers and to young bees.

Recent research suggests that the gummy fluid immobilizes parasitic insects that attack the plant. Some insect species have, however, developed defenses against its effects. These herbaceous insects eat the plant and are then poisonous to their predators.

The latex is also poisonous to cattle. Fortunately, range cattle do not usually eat snow-on-the-mountain. But when the plant is present in hay, cattle can die from the accumulated poison. In addition to containing euphorbon, the plant absorbs selenium from the soil and accumulates it in poisonous amounts.

On the positive side, the latex is caustic enough to be used for branding cattle as a substitute for a hot iron. And the latex from certain spurge species has been considered as a constituent of a rubber substitute and as an energy source.

Snow-on-the-mountain is an annual. Its flowers are borne inside a three to four millimeter-long cup with lobes on its rim. Each lobe is composed of a greenish nectar gland and

Tip of plant

Enlarged flower cup.

an extended white (rarely pink) petal-like appendage. Down inside at the base of the cup are the reproductive flowers. There are from 30 to 60 male flowers in clusters of 15 to 25. At the center is a single female flower which is ready to receive pollen before the male flowers in the cup are ready to provide it. The female flower at this stage reaches just above the rim of the cup within touching distance of the flies and bees arriving to take nectar from the glands at the rim. Some of the pollen clinging to the insects arriving from older flowers is transferred to the female flower and fertilization follows. The female flower's capsule grows and is thrust up beyond the rim of the cup as in a slow motion jack-in-the-box.

The flower stalk, unable to bear the weight of the growing capsule, leans over the edge of the cup. Meanwhile, the male flowers lengthen and make their pollen available at rim height. The difference in maturing time between male and female flowers insures cross-pollination.

When the three light-gray-to-tan seeds inside the capsule are ripe, the capsule snaps open, throwing seeds several meters from the plant. This insures that at least some of the offspring may grow without severe competition from their siblings.

While poisonous to cattle, snow-on-the-mountain is eaten by some prairie mammals and birds. Pronghorns eat the leaves. And from five to ten percent of the diet of mourning doves and greater prairie chickens is spurge seeds. Horned larks also eat the seeds.

The official name of this prairie delight is *Euphorbia marginata* after a celebrated First Century B.C. Greek physician; and the Latin "*marginatus*," in reference to the white margins of its upper leaves.

Prairie Recyclers

Several years ago in the prairie north of Goessel, Jerry and Darlene Schroeder noticed a ring of prairie grasses that were taller and "painted" a deeper green than those inside or outside the circle. With the philosophy "where there is a difference there is a reason," the Schroeders inquired about possible causes. One hypothesis was that the soil producing the taller grasses is enriched by fungi that are digesting the organic matter so abundant in the tallgrass prairie. Perhaps the activity of the fungi released the minerals tied up in the litter and makes them available to surrounding plants. But why the ring?

This year, those prairie circles "blossomed" with mushrooms. These familiar mushrooms are reproductive bodies that form when the scattered threads of a fungus that penetrate soil or wood respond to certain temperature and moisture conditions. Having no chlorophyll, these fungi cannot manufacture food and must survive by producing digestive enzymes. These enzymes break down surrounding organic matter and make available its energy and minerals. The threads absorb some of the digested litter. If an airborne spore released by a mature mushroom alights in the prairie, the spore may germinate and send digestive threads in all directions. If the threads grow at uniform rates, reproductive bodies form periodically at equal distances from their common center to form a "fairy ring."

While some mushrooms are deadly poisonous, others are a gourmet's delight. A local grocer retails ToTo Mushrooms which are produced in a cave at Atchison in northeast Kansas. ToTo cultures the button mushroom (*Agaricus bisporus*) on a mixture of hay, straw, soybean meal, midsol and gypsum. The cave's fairly constant 13°C (56°F) temperature requires no artificial heating or cooling. The cavern was carved out of a 30-acre rock hillside by extracting the limestone.

Probably the only commercial growers in Kansas, ToTo trucks about 9,000 kg (20,000 pounds) of mushrooms out of the abandoned mine each month. The ToTo family was originally involved in mushroom culture in Pennsylvania where most commercially-grown mushrooms of the United States are produced.

Mushrooms, along with molds, smuts, puffballs and bacteria are the great recyclers of the prairie. They digest dead organic matter into forms useable by green plants. Without these recyclers, the bodies of dead creatures would retain their minerals making them unavailable to living creatures. Our prairie would become a desert littered with dead bodies. And there would be no mushroom soup.

The Konza Prairie

The red prairie sun had begun its climb over the rounded knolls of the Flint Hills. We crossed rock-lined Kings Creek and followed the trail to the higher areas of Konza Prairie. Chris Smith, Kansas State University ecologist, interpreted our observations and highlighted ecologic principles illustrated along the trail.

To the left lay the Kansas River Valley. In its floodplain, the Kansa Indians once cultivated corn and squash. Today, descendants of European invaders practice agriculture even more intensely. But up here in the hills, the prairie is largely untouched by the plow. The white limestone rocks and particularly the bands of hard chert (flint) make conventional cultivation impossible. (An example of events occurring in the ancient seas 250 millon years ago affecting our lives today.) So up here, the tallgrass prairie is allowed to flourish.

While the first part of the hike followed a trail always open to the public, most of Konza Prairie's 3487 hectares (8616 acres) are set aside for long-term ecologic research and preservation. They can be visited only with special permission.

The Nature Conservancy purchased the area in 1977. It is managed by KSU's Division of Biology which has divided the prairie into water-shed areas, each with different burning and grazing treatments. This process is designed to study the effects of fire and grazing on the plants, animals and microorganisms of the grasslands. These factors were always significant in the life of the prairie.

Tomorrow would be the last day of summer, so the tall prairie grasses were in full bloom. The soft heads of Indiangrass, the bold turkey feet of big bluestem, the soft tufts of little bluestem, and the loose, spreading heads of switchgrass were standing tall against the eastern sky. Soon the soft reds, purples, and browns of their stalks and leaves would be difficult for even talented artists to reproduce.

Adding to the near-autumn brilliance was the scarlet of smooth sumac. Flowers of prairie roses had by now matured into the bright red fruits called hips ready to provide vitamin C and other nutrients to deer, prairie chickens and other birds and mammals of the Flint Hills.

But in spite of all the fanfare, prairie plants reproduce mostly by spreading roots and rhizomes underground. There is more to the prairie beneath the soil's surface than what we see on top.

Further up the trail, where the soil's surface is farther from the water table, shorter grasses become common. Blue grama, hairy grama, and buffalo grasses are plentiful. Here Chris told us of his student's experiments with the grasses in which voles (prairie rodents) frolic. The student cultured the grasses hydroponically in a solution which excluded silica, the sand that makes most grasses tough and hard. The voles chose the softer grasses for their activities. This supported the long-held hypothesis that the hardness of grasses provided some protection against grazers. Grazers, of course, responded by developing tougher, high-crowned teeth.

From the high hills, we look down on Kings Creek. Along its South Fork lies the native grazer area and we see some of the 90 bison eventually to be joined by elk and pronghorns. For comparison, the watershed of the North Fork is ungrazed.

Kings Creek, says Chris as his eyes survey the valley below, is one of the few watersheds remaining in the Great Plains that originates in an area unaffected by human cultivation. It serves as a basis for comparing the silt-laden streams that our type of agriculture produces.

The public nature trail turns here to descend to Kings Creek and its bur oaks, chinquapin oaks, elms, cottonwoods and willows. The 4.5-km (2.8-mile) portion of the trail is available to anyone of sound body and a bias toward prairie wandering. A printed guide is available to visitors.

Some restricted parts of Konza Prairie are available under supervision on visitors' day, in the fall of even-numbered years.

Kings Creek

The Kansas River winds its way through the fields and forests south of Manhattan receiving waters from numerous prairie streams along the way. One of these is Kings Creek which originates in the upland prairie of the Konza Prairie Research Natural Area. Konza Prairie is a 3,487-hectare (8,616-acre) tract of native tallgrass prairie set aside for long-term ecological research. Since access is restricted, the visitors' day offered in even-numbered years is especially appreciated.

Laura and Karen, prairie ecology students at Kansas State University, lead the last hike of the day. Crossing rocky Kings Creek, we follow bottom land a while and then ascend the grassy slopes to view the Kings Creek watershed from above as it leads to the Kansas River.

Kings Creek cuts through three types of habitat. Over half its length lies in the upland prairie. About a quarter of its route passes through a mixed prairie/shrub habitat. The last quarter of the creek flows through the gallery forest of elms, hackberrys and oaks that shade the creek and absorb a bit of the water for their own use. The variety of habitats greatly multiplies the obvious sights of interest to students of ecology.

With headwaters in the prairie, water in the pools of Kings Creek is clear. What a contrast to the Big Blue River of my childhood. It was always brown from its heavy load of sediment.

It is very near acorn-ripening time. The small fruits of the chinquapin oaks and the large bristly acorns of bur oak are abundant. The red-headed woodpeckers we see may stay for the winter. They emigrate in years when acorns are scarce here.

Near the shrubs along the creek, a conspicuous female black and yellow garden spider clings head-down at the center of its large orb web. Occurring in grasslands, this spider preys on larger jumping and flying insects that carelessly become entangled in the web. Red-legged grasshoppers are a favorite food but their diets also include June beetles and even the meadowland species of cicada heard buzzing in the nearby grassland. Unique in this species' web are the crossed zigzag bands between two adjacent vertical radiating strands above and below the center. The female produces an egg sac with from 400 to 1,200 eggs near the web in September. The young spiders emerge in fall but spend the winter in the sac.

A wood nymph flits among the grasses and shrubs. For food, these butterflies prefer tree sap and decaying fruit. Occasional monarchs fly overhead.

Up the slope are the flowering stalks of big bluestem, Indian grass, switchgrass and taller-than-usual little bluestem. Among the grasses are stenosiphon (an evening primrose) with its long stalk bearing many white flowers, the fruiting heads of moth mullein, the stalks of bright red rose hips, bright yellow goldenrods, the tall and dotted gayfeathers displaying their delightful purple-blue disc flowers, the dark brown curly pod clusters of Illinois bundleflower, the pink globe of the fall-blooming prairie onion, the four tiny white pointed petals of the narrowleaf bluet and the small white blooms and pine-needle leaves of whorled milkweed.

Along rocky ledges are abundant rough-leaved dogwood with their tiny white berries, and smooth sumac with their red-brown fruits and reddening leaves.

The most common forb (any nongrass herb) on Konza is the white heath aster. Asters comprise the largest plant family on Konza, represented by 65 species. Grasses are represented by 55 species. This aster has nickel-size heads, each composed of a disk of yellow florets surrounded by white ray flowers. The cluster, explains Laura, can attract insects more effectively than any flower could alone. Less frequent are the aromatic asters with fewer flower clusters and light purple ray flowers.

Up on the summits, following the trail among the rocks, are buffalo grass and blue grama, even some ragweeds. Laura explains that leaf odor can help distinguish the odorous annual ragweed from the perennial species. Among the rocks, she spots an immature Texas horned lizard which has been described as a miniature dinosaur with its array of spines over its back and around its sides. It eats mostly ants but also takes other small insects and spiders.

It is September 19 and the fall migration of Franklin gulls is in progress (usually September 22 to November 28). Later, I see gulls following a tractor working a field. The gulls swoop down to capture insects, worms and maybe small rodents exposed by the farmer's activity.

In the words of O.J. Reichman, "the tallgrass prairie is a subtle and glorious place that can be appreciated by everyone, regardless of how much they know about biological matters." However, he continues, "the awesome beauty of the prairie is enhanced, not diminished, by knowledge of the prodigious processes that generate the prairie ecosystem."

Harvesting the Osage Orange

Standing apart from the trees lining French Creek is an Osage orange. Its branches intermingle with those of a white mulberry, the two trees occupying the same general space.

If this mulberry bore female flowers, its fruits ripened last spring. But on this last day of summer, the Osage orange is still holding on to its light green, orange-size fruits, called "hedge balls" or "hedge apples." Some hedge branches are so weighted down they almost touch the prairie floor. With an estimated 1,000 fruits that average 200 g per fruit, this tree must be holding 200 kg (90 lbs) of fruits. Not a bad yield for a dry summer. But I have heard of individual trees yielding ten times that much in a good year.

Osage orange, or hedge, trees have been both praised and cursed in the Midwest. In 1867, Kansas farmers were paid to plant hedge fences. In the 1970s, farmers were told that hedge trees destroy the grazing potential of pastures and reduce crop yields by competing aggressively for space, soil moisture and nutrients. And in the 1980s, center-pivot irrigation systems crowded out the hedge rows planted a century ago. More than half the roadside hedges have been destroyed.

A native of Arkansas, Oklahoma, Louisiana, Texas, and possibly southeastern Kansas, the Osage orange was introduced throughout Kansas and beyond to alleviate the fencing problem especially in areas devoid of trees. Its 1.0- to 1.5-cm spines jutting out from the stem allowed the single-row hedges to serve as barbed fences that effectively controlled livestock and seldom required repair. With a two-dollar bounty for each four rods of hedge row planted and a cost of 28 cents, the 43-cent profit per rod encouraged many farmers to fence and cross-fence their farms. And they could sell the fruits at $1.50 per 1,000, or process that number of fruits and sell the resulting bushel of seeds for $25.

In the mid-1870s, after the demise of cattle drives to Abilene, ambitious Baptist, Lutheran and Mennonite immigrants tamed the land with their planting of Osage orange hedge rows.

Known technically as *Maclura pomifera*, the Osage orange is assigned to the mulberry family. Its male and female flowers develop on separate trees. The female flowers grow in dense clusters and mature as an aggregate of many small fruits forming a grapefruit-size, lumpy ball containing a milky juice that turns dark. Its seeds are buried in the sticky flesh.

Native Americans saw special qualities in hedge wood and bark. The Osage and other tribes west of the Mississippi River used the strong flexible wood of the trees for making bows, hence the French name *bois d'arc*, wood of the bow. Such bows were of such superior quality that one of them had the trading value of a pony and blanket. The Comanches prescribed a decoction of the boiled root for treatment of sore eyes. The boiled wood chips and the orange root bark released a yellow pigment used to dye cloth. And tannic acid extracted from the bark of the stem was used in tanning hides.

The present agricultural uses of Osage orange are primarily as live fences, windbreaks and fence posts. Its tolerance of drought and resistance to insects and disease allow it to attain an age of more than 200 years in many areas.

Osage orange wood is known for its hardness, strength, durability, and resistance to bacterial decay. Hence it remains a popular fence post wood, outlasting steel posts by several years. As fossil fuels become less plentiful, its wood may be increasingly used as fuel. Care must be exercised in open fireplaces as it sparks freely. Its hardness, closed grain and beauty make it a good wood for sculpturing.

Most feeding experiments indicate that Osage orange fruits are harmless to livestock. The fruits, however, can cause death in cud-chewers by lodging in the esophagus and preventing the release of ruminal gases.

Nadine Abrahams, as a local junior high school student in 1971, performed experiments which showed no apparent ill effects when she fed the fried fruits to mice, chicks and human subjects. She added other ingredients to mask the bitter taste.

Whether standing alone or in rows, Osage orange trees provide excellent cover and food for songbirds, game birds and mammals. Brown thrashers, mourning doves, catbirds and cardinals often nest in their dense, dark green, waxy foliage. Quail, fox squirrels and eastern cottontails feed on the seeds, leaving piles of fruit pulp as evidence of their activity. Just meters away from this tree, the brushpile den of an eastern wood rat harbors shreds of this year's Osage orange harvest.

Late Summer Along French Creek

The milo field fills the bottom land from French Creek to the north ridge that parallels the stream. Strips of grain have already been harvested, leaving about a third of the crop for wildlife. This native of Africa is not only an important agricultural crop here, but its nutritional value and small kernel size are advantages to a number of local bird species. Studies of animal digestive tracts show that milo constitutes 10 to 25 percent of the diets of bobwhite quail, wild turkey and English sparrows. It makes up five to ten percent of the diets of mallards, lark buntings, and crows and lesser amounts for mourning doves, ring-necked pheasants, redwings, cowbirds, meadowlarks and white-breasted nuthatches. White-tail deer browse on milo leaves and stems.

Near the edges of the field are amaranths as tall as I can reach. Their small shiny, circular seeds provide nourishment to songbirds into the winter when other foods are scarce. They are also eaten by doves, pheasants and quail.

Annual sunflowers are ripe but Maximilian sunflowers are still in full bloom adding brilliance to the field's edge on this overcast afternoon. Their large, nutritious seeds are relished by gamebirds, songbirds and rodents alike.

Common ragweeds are eaten by wildlife but the very abundant giant ragweeds have such large seeds with such tough coats that they are considered of little food value. Their leaves, however, are eaten by white-tailed deer.

Some goldenrods still display a rich golden-yellow while others are already fruiting. Their seeds are eaten in small quantities by songbirds and their foliage by beaver, porcupine, eastern cottontails and game birds.

The Pennsylvania smartweed, now with pink blossoms, by winter will produce seeds for waterfowl and many songbirds.

Virginia groundcherry's bladders are still green. The blossoms of flower-of-an-hour are closing from this morning's bloom.

Among the smartweeds and groundcherries at the base of the ridge are dozens of small butterflies I am unable to identify. A few familiar monarchs flit at higher altitudes. Here too are stalks of Indian grass, its tan plumes reaching skyward. Here and there are deer tracks.

The wild plums covering the ridge have finished their fruiting season, not a hint of their fruits left. While not important as food for wildlife, these thickets offer protective shelter. Blue jays and brown thrashers are here today. As I walk along the base of the ridge, the whistling wings of mourning doves suggest their use of the thicket as cover.

Later in the evening, mounting a hill south of the South Cottonwood River, two great blue herons appear suddenly as if having taken off just over the slope. Stomach contents of 189 of these large wading birds are about 43 percent nongame fish, 25 percent gamefish, 8 percent insects, 8 percent crayfish and their relatives, 5 percent mice and shrews, and 4 percent frogs, snakes and turtles.

Seeing these magnificent birds against the brilliant red of the western sky provides an inspiring close to a beautiful day and the end of a long summer.

FALL

The Colors of Autumn

Whether viewing the deciduous forests that clothe the Arbuckle Mountains of Oklahoma, the drainage creeks of Konza Prairie in the Flint Hills, or the banks of Cub Creek in Nebraska, the splash of fall colors is as much a part of autumn as is the annual dropping of leaves from trees and shrubs.

The splendor of these autumn colors is due to chemical changes. As days get shorter and nights get cooler, a layer of corky tissue forms where a tree leaf fastens to the twig. The water, necessary for the continuous rebuilding of chlorophyll, can no longer enter or exit the leaf freely. The chlorophyll now decomposes faster than it is made. As the green chlorophyll disappears, the yellow and yellow-orange colors appear. They were present all summer but were dominated by the chlorophyll. These yellows are obvious in autumn cottonwoods and elms.

There are other colors, too. In many species, if fall days are sunny and the nights cool, the leaves continue making sugar as long as chlorophyll lasts. The accumulating sugar reacts with various minerals to form red and purple pigments. The leaves of smooth sumac turn red under these conditions.

The brown color of dead leaves is due to the death of tissues and the production of tannins in the leaf.

The corky tissue formed at the base of the leaf stalk forms a plane of weakness where the leaf most easily breaks off. This loss of leaves, as one might guess, fulfills a function for perennial plants in Earth's temperate zones. Here in the Midwest, winter is usually a dry season. Food-making requires water, and low humidity results in water loss by rapid evaporation from leaves. Losing leaves reduces both demands for water.

The flashy combinations of autumn reds and yellows may attract our aesthetic attention but the green of chlorophyll is more significant to the life of the ecosystem. It is the chlorophyll that performs the major task of absorbing the light energy required to power the process of food-making. And this food-making, called photosynthesis, forms the base of the food chain. On this conversion of solar energy into chemical energy in the leaf depends the existence of plants and the creatures that eat plants and the creatures that eat plant-eaters. So the coyote that eats the rabbit that eats the clover is also indebted to the clover's ability to convert solar energy into chemical, or food, energy. And so is the vulture or the bacterium that feeds on a dead coyote.

So, intellectually, we should be as excited about the greens of spring and summer as we are about the reds and yellows of fall.

Have you thanked a green plant today?

How Birds Fly

The other day, I saw a great blue heron plow steadily across the prairie sky. There is something grand about these great birds in flight. Perhaps it is their ability to fly. Flight clearly distinguishes birds from most other creatures. Only insects and bats rival birds in this attainment.

Birds' ability to fly generates both mystery and envy in the human spirit. Flight is one of the four wonders of the world mentioned in the Biblical book of Proverbs (30:19). A survey of native children in Africa reveals that nearly half the boys and a quarter of the girls want to be birds. This suggests a desire to escape the trials of their earthbound existence.

Indeed, flight allows birds to escape threatening predators and unpleasant seasonal conditions. It increases opportunities to get food and to travel vast distances and over great barriers to more desirable living and breeding areas.

But just how do birds fly? The answer to that question had to await the invention of the airplane. To fly, both birds and airplanes need lift and forward thrust. In birds, both lift and thrust are supplied by their wings.

A bird's body is heavier than air and depends on two forces to overcome gravity. One I call the kite effect. A kite, or a wing, is pulled through the air at some incline (angle of attack) so that the bottom of the wing pushes against the air. According to Newton's third law of motion, if the wing pushes against the air, the air pushes back against the wing with an equal force in the opposite direction. The upward component of this force creates about one quarter of the lift of a typical airplane wing.

The other three-quarters of the wing's lift results from its cross-sectional shape. The Swiss mathematician Daniel Bernoulli discovered that where a fluid flows fastest, its internal pressure is least. If the wing is shaped so that air stream traveling over the wing must travel farther and, therefore, faster than that under the wing, the air pressure against the top of the wing will be less than that against the bottom. If the upper surface of the bird's wing is arched and the lower surface is flat, and the entire wing is tilted as it is pulled through the air, the greater air pressure under the wing will overcome the downward pull of gravity.

But this all assumes that the bird's wings are moving forward through the air. In an airplane, forward thrust is generated by either a propeller or a jet engine. A propeller is really a set of wings repositioned to produce "lift" in a forward direction.

In birds, the flight feathers that extend out from the tips of wings function as propellers. The stiff quill of a flight feather lies toward its leading edge. The leading edge of the feather is, therefore, narrower and the trailing edge is wider. And since the feather can twist around its axis, vertical motion of the entire feather results in pushing air back whether the wing moves up or down. Either way, air is pushing the flight feathers forward and the rest of the bird follows.

The heron's flight across the blue prairie sky recalls the poetic words of Joel Peters, "O, for the Wings of a Bird!"

• • •

Prairie observers enjoy the contrasts between the great eagles and dainty hummingbirds, the plain crow and gaudy painted bunting, the trill of a house wren and honk of a goose, the mating antics of a prairie chicken and a song sparrow.

Birds do differ considerably in size, color, song, and behavior. But they are far more uniform in body features than mammals are. The largest living mammal (blue whale) weighs 59,000,000 times as much as the smallest (pigmy shrew). The largest living bird (ostrich) weighs only about 66,000 times as much as the smallest (hummingbird).

The similarity among birds in body architecture is even more striking. This similarity is required by the demands of flight. The universal presence of wings in birds provides both uplift and forward thrust. The kite effect and Bernoulli's principle require a fairly specific aerodynamic design.

Additional requirements of flight were noted as early as 1679 by Italian physiologist Borelli; reduced weight and high power.

Since animals that fly must overcome the pull of gravity, any feature that reduces body weight should make flight easier—as long as strength and movement aren't sacrificed. Take bones, for example. The skeleton of a pigeon accounts for only 4.4 percent of its body weight. That of rat accounts for 5.6 percent. In birds, more bones are thin and hollow. The hip bones and several vertebrae of the backbone are molded together into a light, but strong, tube. Some hollow bones of the legs, wings, and skull contain internal truss-like reinforcements that strengthen those thin structures, eliminating the need for solid bone.

Birds have eliminated some structures partially or completely. The body covering of scales seen in reptiles is replaced by much lighter feathers in birds. Teeth are thrown overboard; consequently the heavy bones and muscles for biting and chewing are reduced in birds. The only skin glands that birds retain are oil glands.

Much of the water we drink is excreted through our kidneys to dilute urea, the substance formed from our nitrogenous wastes. In birds, nitrogenous wastes are eliminated in the form of white uric acid crystals, and they are eliminated often. This not only reduces the need for water; it also eliminates the need of a urinary bladder and a urethra to contain and discharge urine.

Most mammals give birth to live young which have developed through time inside the mother's body. All species of birds incubate eggs outside the mother's body soon after the eggs are fertilized.

Since birds have a definite breeding season, adults are burdened with heavy sex organs for only part of the year. In starlings, both ovaries and testes decrease in size during the non-breeding season. These organs weigh 1500 times as much during the breeding season as they do the rest of the year.

Birds conserve weight even in the foods they select. They eat seeds, fruits, worms, insects, rodents, fish, and other calorie-rich foods. They reject leaves and other bulky, low-calorie foods.

Another weight-related factor is the rapid digestion of foods. A domestic chicken requires 12 to 24 hours to digest a cropful of grain. But a shrike can digest a mouse in three hours. A thrush defecates the seeds 30 minutes after eating the fruits of elderberry. Berry seeds appear in the wastes of young cedar waxwings in 16 minutes.

The net effect of all these weight-reducing features is striking. The body of a duck weighs only six-tenths as much as an equal volume of most vertebrate bodies.

Light weight, and wings that supply lift and thrust have produced a group of creatures that have achieved success not only in the prairie but over much of the planet.

●　　●　　●

Two glistening-white birds with black primary wing feathers and great orange bills were flying leisurely toward the upper reaches of Marion Reservoir. A fitting sight on this first half day of autumn (September 22), these American white pelicans were the first signs of their fall migration which usually peaks in late September and early October.

Miraculously, these great birds are able to spread their nearly three-meter wing span to fly from North Dakota or Minnesota to the Gulf Coast. But the relatively light weight of a bird and the presence of wings providing lift and thrust would be ineffective without a force moving these wings. And birds have assembled an impressive array of adaptations that provide the power for flight.

It is the great muscles of the breast that move a bird's wings. In superior fliers like swallows, doves, and ducks, these flight muscles make up 25 to 35 percent of the total body weight. The outermost breast muscle attaches to the blade of the breastbone and to the underside of the arm bone some distance from the shoulder joint. Its contraction lowers the wing.

To lift the wing one might expect a muscle on the backbone; but that would raise the bird's center of weight and make its position less stable. Instead, the muscle that raises the wing is also located under the wing just inside the muscle that lowers the wing. It, too, originates on the blade of the breastbone but ends in a tendon that passes up through an opening in the shoulder bones, turns outward and downward to insert on the upper surface of the arm bone. When this inner breast muscle contracts, the tendon, like a rope and pulley system, pulls up on the arm bone.

In domestic birds, the breast muscles are white. In birds that use their breast muscles for flight, the muscles are more richly supplied with blood capillaries and are red.

Birds have a high rate of metabolism; that is, they live intensely. Some sparrows and thrushes have body temperatures of 42° to 43°C (107° to 110°F), compared to the human 37°C. Chemical reactions occur faster at higher temperatures. Without consistently high body temperatures, flight would be impossible in cool climates. And this warm-bloodedness, in turn, would be impossible without an insulating coat of feathers.

The oxygen and fuel delivery system in birds is impressive. Birds, like mammals, pump blood with four-chambered hearts. All of the blood takes a side trip through the lungs for gaseous purification before it is circulated through the body. In amphibians and reptiles there is a mixing of oxygenated and deoxygenated bloods. The human heart beats about 75 times per minute; in vultures, crows, and hummingbirds the rate is 300, 340, and 600 beats per minute, respectively. Blood pressure is also somewhat higher in birds. Blood sugar concentration in birds is about twice that in mammals.

Birds have highly efficient respiratory systems. Communicating with their lungs is a system of usually five pairs of air sacs. Branches of these sacs, in turn, penetrate the hollows of larger bones. Experiments indicate that there is essentially a one-way stream of air through the lungs. In mammals, the mixing of stale and fresh air with each breath into dead-end lungs is inefficient.

We have already mentioned the consumption of energy-rich foods as a contribution to low weight. (Our pelicans feed almost entirely on fish.) Rich foods also insure power for flight. Rapid and efficient digestion, likewise, serve both to reduce weight and produce power for flight.

Birds are also more efficient energy consumers. Field and laboratory studies show that flying birds are 10 to 25 times as energy efficient as walking or running mammals of the same size. This efficiency makes it possible for birds to fly non-stop about 4000 km (2500 miles) as they migrate over oceans and deserts.

Gould Creek

Gould Creek cuts under Kansas Highway 150 about 5.6 km (3.5 miles) west-southwest of the Flint Hills town of Elmdale. It originates on the grassy slopes within the first kilometer north of the highway and meanders southeast through Clover Cliff Ranch for about four kilometers (2.5 miles) until it reaches the Cottonwood River. Here the river loops northwest in a horseshoe curve to meet the creek and receive its runoff from occasional prairie rains.

From this vantage point at the headwaters of Gould Creek, we see rounded hills of short-cropped grasses with mats of yellow-blooming broomweed and occasional clumps of cottonwoods, willows and elms along the creek. We stand here with a few blooming ruellia among piles of fresh soil pushed to the surface by plains pocket gophers.

A pool of water stands next to the highway culvert which protects one barn swallow nest plastered against its inside wall.

The creek bed is dry and rocky with false indigo and broomweed in and along its course.

Scattered white sage, American elms and black willows follow further along.

Here the creek waters have eroded through the limestone into shale, leaving a cattle-trampled area. A field cricket scampers across the dried mud.

A small limestone rock covered with fossilized fusilinids, like a large handful of petrified wheat grains, reminds us of a time when this drying prairie was a shallow sea. Its load of minerals settled out to form the alternating layers of limestone and shale whose edges were exposed by the erosive action of water rushing down the slopes. From here, we can see two tiers of limestone exposed on the slopes across the creek—probably Morrill and Cottonwood Limestones.

Now larger rocks are exposed in the creek bed. Whether flat on the ground or perched in lifted position, they are fractured into chunks one meter long, a half meter wide and fifteen centimeters thick. A black and yellow garden spider crawls on a rock. This spider spins its large orb web among tall prairie grasses and shrubs and captures insects such as cicadas, June beetles and red-legged grasshoppers. Even young garter snakes have become entangled in its webs and eaten by the spider.

A meadowlark takes flight from near a lone goldenrod. A poison ivy grows from a space between two layers of limestone, its leaves turning a yellow-red. On the rock face of the creek bank, buckbrush holds up its small red berries among the dogwoods with their leaves also turning a deep red.

Downcreek, four greater prairie chickens are disturbed by my presence and run across the creek for cover in the rocks and shrubs. Swallows glide by, collecting their morning meal of airborne insects. In the rock-free flats of the creek bottom, a tiny-leaved matting spurge attempts to cover the bare soil. Its leaves are also turning red.

On the west bank, among the rocks are aromatic sumacs, called skunk bush because of the odor of their crushed leaves. Eastern wood rats often build their dens at the base of these shrubs and eat their bark in winter.

At the base of the limestone bluff is a grove of 17 Kentucky coffee trees with their bulky brown pods that will hang on all winter. Out in the clearing, a female ornate box turtle crawls toward the creek. And over the hill, an Aermotor Windmill comes into view, delivering water to a stock tank. Several cattle stand around, drinking their fill before munching more grasses.

Overhead, two turkey vultures glide on air currents and a red-tailed hawk screams.

From the west, a tributary enters Gould Creek. The creek bottom here is bare soil. I collect a few clam shells identified as *Ligumia subrostrata* by Don Huggins of the Kansas Biological Survey. This species is common in our small streams. Sperm from the male are released into the surrounding water and collected, by chance, by females. Soon after fertilization, the developing embryo is released by the female to parasitize a fish. Adult organs form within a month and the larva breaks off, falls to the creek bottom and develops into an adult clam. This process may take several years—nature's lesson in patience.

In the open landscape away from the creek, a male ornate box turtle ambles across the stubby grasses.

I see clumps of little bluestem. But of all the tall prairie grasses I've seen along Gould Creek, none have flowers or fruits today. During this dry summer, the scattered cattle need all the grass they get. But there are only a few ironweeds, those symptoms of overgrazing.

Not all cattle on the range survive. Here are the bleached bones of one cow or steer strewn among the grasses. The skull and pelvis lie 15 m from the vertebral column, ribs and jawbones. Some prairie creatures have gained their livelihood at the expense of another.

It's time to move on; I've gone only halfway to the river.

•   •   •

From the uplands of Clover Cliff Ranch, a bit down the slope is a circular stone wall. It is about five meters in diameter, a half to one meter high and surrounds two mid-age eastern cottonwoods. It is late September, 26 days after Tim Donahue pointed out this structure while delivering salt blocks to grazing cattle. No one remembers, or ever knew, the purpose of the wall.

Immediately down the slope, toward the southwest at another outcrop, is a seep. Water is oozing into stagnant pools supporting broad-leaved cattails, common bulrush (its tops eaten off), watercress, an aquatic marigold and floating duckweeds. This oasis is the first water I've seen since leaving the "headwaters" of Gould Creek, three kilometers to the northwest.

Forty meters downstream, the water heading for Gould Creek dries up. The upper shell of a common snapping turtle bleaching in the sun is another reminder of this dry summer.

Continuing along Gould Creek, the first common buttonbush appears. Up the slope, among the chunks of pock-marked limestone, I see the fall-red leaves of smooth sumac. Under a rock ledge, are violets, shaded from direct sunlight.

I walk back, away from the rocks on higher ground, and see prickly pear cactus with glistening green pads. There are scattered chunks of chert, or flint, from which these Flint Hills derive their name.

As the sun crosses the zenith, I descend to Gould Creek which is now entering a forested area. Again there are black willows and American elms. Still buckbrush and smooth sumac. But also honey locusts, green ash and sycamores about twice my height growing in the creek bottom. The trees high up on the south bank cast their welcome shade on this portion of the creek.

Debris snagged at twice my height up in ash trees suggests that this land that experiences drought sees floods as well.

A great horned owl wings its way among the tree tops. Here below, six wild turkeys retreat up the south slope.

I pass a snow-on-the-mountain, shoulder-height—the tallest I've ever seen.

I hurry across an empty corral, follow the creek under U.S. Highway 50, and under the Santa Fe Railroad bridge. Below the railroad bridge is a stagnant pool dark-green with algae. Tracks of wild turkey, deer and other creatures are crowded in the mud near the pool.

In this section of Gould Creek, I see Pennsylvania smartweed, mapleleaf goosefoot, giant ragweed (in bloom), pokeberry and white snakeroot. Snakeroot displays its small white flowers from July into November in open woods and frequently-moist stream bottoms. While attractive, the plant does contain a poison that causes illness in cattle and can be transferred, through a cow's milk, to humankind, causing nausea, weakness and collapse.

In the dry creek bottom is an empty shell of another common snapping turtle. A fox squirrel scampers up a bur oak.

At 12:30 p.m., I stand on the bank of a very dry Gould Creek where it "empties" into the Cottonwood River. Flanked by an American elm and a green ash, the empty creek watches as a few fallen leaves float down the Cottonwood at about one meter per nine seconds. A common flicker flies among the trees.

Hiking downstream, I had cut through successively lower and older layers of Earth's crust. Now, in returning upstream, I reconstruct history, rebuilding those sedimentary strata until I reach the higher and more recent levels of these Flint Hills.

I pick and eat a few Virginia ground cherries and head west to get a closer view of the stone house at Clover Cliff.

Up against the bluff, I see the two-story structure built in 1883 by J.R. Blackshere who established the ranch in 1860. It attracted the attention of the poet Vachel Lindsay in 1912 on one of his walking tours from his home in Illinois to New Mexico, according to author William Least Heat-Moon.

Clover Cliff is listed in the National Registry of Historical Sites and is currently being restored by Wes and Rosella Seibel for owners Jim and Joan Donahue of Lincolnville.

At the base of the bluff, Dutch Talkington and Bobby Hokyr are building a steel fence. Dutch is employed at Clover Cliff as were his father and grandfather before him. I explained my presence, chat a bit and mount the bluff to head back to the "headwaters" of Gould Creek.

I walk north toward the pond southwest of the creek. A turkey vulture glides overhead, wings outstretched but never flapping.

I rest a while, lying in a depression that matches my contours. I munch on sunflower seeds from my pack.

Grasshoppers are plentiful here; many differential and red-winged grasshoppers. I see one lubber grasshopper, large but without functional wings. In their place is a pair of small pads, useless for flight. These grasshoppers do well during dry years.

Moving on to higher ground, another prickly pear cactus appears among the grasses. A small, white cottony mass on the cactus pad catches my eye. This is the protective coating of a cochineal insect that feeds on cactus juices. As I squeeze the mass, its deep-red cochineal coats my finger. I imagine a Plains Indian decorating his face and arms with the dye. More recently, cochineal was used to dye textiles, foods and cosmetics. One can't wander far in the prairie without finding another of nature's surprises.

I'm still wondering about that circular stone wall.

The Sauble Cabin at Cedar Creek

Two human figures stood on the roadside across from the stone barn in Chase County's Cedar Creek valley. Engraved in a gable stone of the barn were the words "D. Sauble 1876." Artist Jim Gates of nearby Cedar Point was sketching the barn, black on white. Ed Frikes, a retired California teacher, was working on color paintings.

Jim seemed familiar with local family history. The white frame house among the trees up the slope had been built in 1871. The rubble beside the driveway, he said, represents the chimney and log remains of the original Sauble cabin built earlier. A tunnel led from the cabin to a nearby well in case the Saubles were besieged by hostile natives. The only natives they encountered turned out to be friendly, according to Mary Sauble. Her husband, Pat, is pioneer David Sauble's grandson. The log cabin, according to Pat, was actually an old trapper's cabin built before 1850.

David Sauble, continued Mary, was killed by lightning when Pat's father, John, was 16 years old. The boy stayed home to manage the ranch while his mother moved with her other sons to Manhattan so they could attend the state college.

Mary suggested that housekeeping by 16-year-old John and the ranch hands was neglected in favor of ranch work. So it is easy to imagine the story Pat related to William Least Heat-Moon in *PrairyErth*. Hearing footsteps on the stairway leading to his bedroom one night, John grabbed his gun and proceeded cautiously to the head of the stairway. The intruder was a wood rat struggling down the stairs tugging a gunnysack that contained a few potatoes.

Mary hopes that Pat takes time from his ranch work to record other stories he has heard or experienced here along Cedar Creek.

Lobelias Along a Spring Brook

The first light snow of the season has melted. A haze has settled in the valleys of the Smoky Hills and the tall prairie grasses cover the rounded summits with their hues. Here and there, the white tufts of little bluestem glisten against the afternoon sun of early October. The valley floor is carpeted with patches of goldenrod whose seeds are ready for dispersal. Occasional flowering heads of aromatic asters appear among the grasses.

Daughter Kris and I tramp along the marshy edge of the spring brook that leads to a box canyon. Here, the lobelias are in full bloom. The great blue lobelia I've seen here before. But the red one, known as cardinal flower, I see here for the first time.

The cardinal flower, officially *Lobelia cardinalis*, is an herbaceous perennial found from Quebec to Florida. It ranges from 0.2 to 1.5 meters in height. Its bright scarlet flowers have been described as "perhaps untouched in brilliance by any other of our wildflowers." They are arranged along a tall stalk.

The flower of this species is three to four centimeters long, tubular at its base, but divides into two lips farther out. The upper lip is two-lobed; the lower is three-lobed.

In a freshly-opened flower, the five male stamens are united into a tube which surrounds and caps the central female pistil. As the flower opens, this stamen-pistil complex lengthens and turns down. At this stage, the pollen has been deposited on a collar of hairs which keeps the pollen from reaching the inner stigmatic surface, preventing self-fertilization. Hummingbirds or hawk moths arriving at this stage can, unknowingly, take pollen from the collar and transfer it to an older flower in which the stigmatic surface is exposed and ready to allow cross-fertilization. The nectar these animals seek is secreted down inside the tube of stamens.

All parts of a lobelia plant are toxic due to the presence of several alkaloids. Early European invaders learned from the Native Americans how to use them to make medicines for a variety of disorders. Eighteenth and nineteenth century physicians in the United States and Europe used the species as a cathartic and an emetic. Cherokees used the root to treat worm infestations. The Meskwakis used its roots as a "love medicine," believing it to avert divorce. Human deaths sometimes resulted from misuse of this plant.

Kris and I also enjoyed the bright blue blossoms of the big blue lobelia. It, too, is perennial and is 0.2 to 0.9 m tall. Its flowers have nearly the same characteristics as those of the red species, except for color. It was used medicinally for many of the same disorders.

The Iroquois and Cherokees used the root of the big blue lobelia to treat venereal diseases. As its official name *Lobelia siphilitica* implies, it was reputed to cure syphilis, especially when fresh material was used together with certain other plants. Some doubted its value in treating syphilis but believed it was effective against gonorrhea.

While the medicinal use of these species has diminished, their value as ornamentals in flower gardens persists. And the intense scarlet and bright blue of their flowers along this stream deepen our appreciation of the Smoky Hills of central Kansas.

The Flint Hills at Stribby Creek

The rounded hills between Stribby Creek and the Chase-Marion County line seem especially majestic on this warm mid-October afternoon. The mature bluestem and Indian grasses spread their mosaic of soft yellows, reds and purples over the Flint Hills as they do each fall. The earlier bright blossoms of heath aster and blazing star are now white fuzzies being dispatched by the wind. Patches of buckbrush display their dark red fruits, half hidden among their green leaves.

Down the slope, along an outcropping of loose limestone rocks, stands an isolated Osage orange tree. I noticed it on an earlier hike and came today to investigate what appears to be the nest of an eastern woodrat supported by the lower branches of the tree. About three meters off the ground, the globular nest is about a meter in diameter and is composed of dry twigs and pieces of bark. Among the rocks at the base of the gnarled trunk of this hedge tree, are white sage, common ragweeds, and a single acorn. There are no clear signs of current habitation of the nest, unless the acorn was dropped by a woodrat while bringing food for winter storage.

There are no "hedge apples"—this tree must have borne male flowers. Or if it bore female flowers, this isolated tree may not have received pollen from male trees up wind.

Further down the slope, in the trough between hills, a spring flows from a limestone outcropping and supplies fresh water to a little pool. My presence startles a small bullfrog in the pool. It quickly swims to the protection of an overhanging limestone slab.

Water striders are "skating" on the water's surface. What appear to be crawling water beetles are walking along the pool's bottom and swimming in its clear water. Floating in the water are strands of stonewort, brittle "stems" with whorls of branches at regular intervals. These green algae are found in pools fed by waters from limestone soils. Their limy covering discourages being eaten; but they harbor multitudes of tiny water creatures plus wintering water bugs, water striders, and water boatmen. Crawling water beetles actually feed on stoneworts and other filamentous green algae such as *Spirogyra*, also seen here. With this potential food supply, it's no wonder the bullfrog is content in this small pool.

Down stream where chunks of chert fall from the loosely constructed limestone layer, the swampy edge of the stream is inhabited by sedges, spikerush, and lobelias holding up their ripening fruits.

Further along, the brook leads toward Stribby Creek (Strawberry Creek on my State Geological Survey map). Nearing the creek, bur oaks stand around on a rocky flat, holding on to their few remaining acorns. Along the creek itself, the oaks are joined by elms, hackberries, green ash, black walnut, and sycamores with their patchy trunks. The autumn-red leaves of smooth sumac brighten the understory of the gallery forest.

While there are pools of standing water in Stribby, longer stretches of dry, flat rock bottom occur. Covering much of the flat bedrock is a recently flourishing moss and a filamentous alga. Now they lie flattened against the rock, abandoned by the water that nourished them.

Before taking leave of this autumn scene, I mount the nearest summit. Up here in the brisk wind, the uplands support predominantly little bluestem, blue grama, and sideoats grama. A single prickly pear cactus offers its sweet, red, slimy fruits.

From this vantage point, I see the tree-lined creek make its way from the northern horizon to the south where, according to my map, it joins Middle Creek. And Middle Creek directs its prairie waters into the Cottonwood River near Elmdale.

As silent as the meadowlarks here today, the Flint Hills portray a certain quiet majesty. They lift their rounded pieces of tallgrass prairie skyward calling attention to its beauty and grandeur.

This has been a good afternoon.

Homesteading at Cub Creek

The crisp October night was pitch black. The distant stars generated just enough light to reveal the roadside fence. I entered the open gate into a field or pasture and unrolled my sleeping bag under a medium sized tree that offered its leafless shelter for the cool night to follow. I had come back to my childhood community for a conference and decided to spend the night under the stars.

I didn't know whose land I wandered onto. I knew only that it was near the Dan

Freeman homestead on the banks of Cub Creek in Gage County, Nebraska.

Cub Creek drained the glaciated farmland of southeast Nebraska. It passed by Herman Schmale's dugout, cut through my grandparent's farm, meandered across Freeman's homestead and finally joined the Big Blue River near Beatrice.

Thirty-five years earlier, I had worked for the farmer who contracted the mowing of the grassland on this 160-acre homestead. Our horse-drawn mowers found the stems and leaves of tall prairie grasses to be tough and wiry. We often stopped to replace worn blades on the sicklebar.

By this time, the Freeman homestead had been purchased by the Federal government to commemorate the Homestead Act of 1862 which provided 160 acres to settlers who paid a minor fee, built a house and cultivated the land for five years. Dan Freeman had quickly reserved this plot in the early hours of January 1, 1863, so that he could get back to his job as secret agent for the Union army.

Following the Civil War, grizzly-bearded Freeman returned to this homestead where he and his wife, Agnes, farmed and raised their family. During hard times, Dan took to his horse and practiced frontier medicine.

But Freeman must have had his good years. He even had a little money to invest. As a minor partner with a local horse fancier, Freeman bought a $10,000 Arabian stallion that had been given to President U.S. Grant by the Sultan of Turkey. Grant gave his horse to his son who sold it to Freeman and his partner. Expecting to raise fancy racing stock, the pair set up a race track near Beatrice. They called it Linden Tree Park after the stallion, named Zeizefoan, Turkish for Linden Tree. The blue-gray stallion was a fine trotter but had a hostile disposition and never reached the expectations of its owners. The horse was given a royal burial in the straw-lined grave at the center of Linden Tree Park, just across the fence from my family home. The farm that replaced the race track became known as Linden Tree Park Farm, although as a child I never knew why.

Meanwhile, the Freeman homestead was experiencing severe erosion of its upland slopes and silt was deposited on bottomlands and in Cub Creek. Woodlands were being cut and heavily grazed. When Mother's family rode by in their carriage, they noted the rundown condition of the homestead. Only old-timers remembered that the Big Blue River was once really blue. But now, silt from Freeman's homestead and other farms in the valley was being carried down the Blue and through Kansas, Missouri and Mississippi Rivers to the Gulf of Mexico.

When the U.S. Congress set this plot aside as the Homestead National Monument in 1939, management was aimed at "stabilizing the severely abused soil and protecting newly planted native grasses." In August of 1988, when the Eleventh North American Prairie Conference met in Nebraska, I joined the field trip to the homestead to inspect the progress of prairie reconstruction efforts. This, we were told, is one of the oldest ongoing prairie restorations on a human-abused landscape. Sodding, seeding, mowing, spraying and burning are management tools that have been used here. And slowly, prairie conditions are returning to this early homestead.

Long-standing abuse of the prairie is not easily overcome.

What Is It?

What is it? This is a common question folks ask when they bring me a creature unfamiliar to them.

I may not know what it is without referring to an appropriate manual or checking with an expert on that group of organisms. After all, there are over 10,000 species of just ants. No one can recognize them all on sight.

But it is interesting to see how easily people are satisfied when they are given only the name of an organism without further information. Biologist Marsten Bates wonders if there is "some lingering element of word magic here, some feeling that knowing the name gives you power over the thing named—the sort of feeling that leads members of some savage tribes to conceal their personal names from all except their intimates. An enemy hearing their name might be able to use this power for some evil purpose."

Being satisfied with the name of a creature is like planning a vacation trip to some exotic place, and then being satisfied with a roadmap.

A creature's name is indeed a roadmap to further information; where it lives, what it eats, what eats it, how it solves its problems, its role in its ecosystem, how it relates to other creatures we know. While these facts can be learned through field and laboratory observations, we can save time by relying on the previous observations of others if we know the creature's name. Then we can turn our efforts to new questions not yet answered. Furthermore, with its name we can search the literature for folk uses of the organism. Folk uses fall beyond the scope of field and laboratory analysis.

I remember seeing the striking blossom of a cardinal flower back in August of 1972. It was near the mouth of Sand Creek, a tributary of the South Ninnescah River in Kingman County. The unique features of its flowers attracted my attention and identified it as *Lobelia cardinalis*. One botanist observes that the "bright scarlet flowers are perhaps unmatched in brilliance by any other of our wildflowers."

Several years later, I observed the species in September in a Marion County roadside ditch and again near a tributary of French Creek. In October of 1992 it appeared in the Smoky Hills along the marshy edge of a spring brook.

The Great Plains Floral Association and Janét Bare contribute detailed information including cross-pollination mechanisms. They relate the species to other similar ones, placing it into the bellflower family. Melvin Gilmore, who interviewed many elderly Pawnee Indians, reports it as a component of their love charms. Virgil Vogel lists numerous medicinal uses of the species by Native Americans.

Homer Stephens lists the symptoms of poisoning of humans and livestock by the cardinal flower's alkaloids such as lobelamine and lobeline. Kelly Kinscher notes that lobeline hydrochloride is used in the resuscitation of newborn infants. Lobeline is an ingredient in several commercial products that help people quit smoking as it acts similar to nicotine in exciting and paralyzing nerve cells. Kinscher cautions against its use as a home remedy, however, because fatal overdoses have resulted from its improper use.

Without the proper name of the cardinal flower none of this information would be available to me. And it would require years to acquire it personally. Think of the state of our technology if we had to re-invent the wheel each generation.

But those who are satisfied with only the name of this species, miss most of the advantages that name has to offer.

The Lake Takes a Deep Breath

Now that Earth's North Pole is leaning progressively farther away from the sun, temperatures in the mid-latitude grasslands are chilling. And the water in Marion Reservoir is following that trend. Folks that fish know that this seasonal change is important to the survival of creatures in our lakes and ponds, especially the deeper ones.

During summers, the oxygen dissolved in the bottom water has been depleted by the bacteria of decay as they digest dead fish and other debris in the bottom mud. The warmer well-oxygenated waters at the top of the lake are lighter and remain in their floating position, always exposed to the Midwest winds.

But in the fall, as the surface water cools down, it shrinks. Becoming more dense, it sinks and takes its load of oxygen to the bottom. The lake has taken a deep breath.

Most substances keep shrinking as they cool. But water is an exception. It becomes more dense as it cools only until it reaches 4°C (39°F). As it continues to cool down from 4°C, water expands. So it no longer sinks. By now, the whole body of water has reached 4°C. As surface water cools to 0°C, the water begins freezing at the top of the lake or pond. But the water has received its annual fall oxygen supply and water creatures can survive until spring, even with periodic ice cover.

The heat of the summer also affects water creatures. My boyhood friend, Elroy Springer, lived in the wooded edge of the Big Blue River in southeast Nebraska. His father farmed a few patches of rich bottomland. When the volume of runoff from late spring rains exceeded the river's capacity, its muddy waters spread over the Springers' fields and woodlands. As waters receded, small pools abandoned by the main stream sometimes trapped fish.

Unshaded pools with black mud bottoms absorbed the full heat of the sun. And since high temperatures diminish the ability of water to contain dissolved gases, the dissolved oxygen supply was soon depleted. At the same time, high temperatures caused the metabolic rate of fish to speed up, increasing their oxygen use. So the fish suffocated, drowned, unless Elroy returned the fish to the river.

The survival of water creatures depends on the natural processes that surround them. As needed resources diminish or wastes accumulate, creatures either migrate or perish.

As I wander through the open prairie or follow wooded streams, I realize that humankind, too, is subject to these restraints. But migration becomes less of an option as the human population continues to grow and degrade its home planet. And there aren't many livable planets in our solar system. It may well be that we will have to learn to live on this one. Let's hope that we are fast learners.

Planet Earth in Crisis

It was early November and we were making our way north parallel to the Washita River in south-central Oklahoma. The rounded summits of the Arbuckle Mountains were coated with clumps of deciduous trees, each species displaying its characteristic yellow, copper, green, or red. Roadcuts exposed sharply slanting strata of granite and limestone, telling the story of extreme stress in Earth's crust a half billion years ago when these mountains pushed up from the sediment-filled basin. The once-tall peaks have since eroded to a mere 200 meters above the surrounding plains.

A day earlier, I had stood on the 24th level of Houston's Hotel Westin Galleria and surveyed the bustling city. The distant encircling horizon held a million gray-brown buildings and a tangled web of flowing roadways. I wondered if the human population represented by this scene might be even more stressful to our home planet than were the stresses that wrinkled and warped Earth's crust as the Arbuckles pushed tortuously skyward.

The theme of the convention that brought us to Houston was "Planet Earth in Crisis: How Do We Respond?" And respond we must! Either deliberately, or with reckless abandonment and consequent annihilation.

It is humbling to realize that Earth's other critters can survive *without* us. And perhaps they will survive only without us. We are already degrading our planet at a rate that will destroy an estimated million species in the next 25 years—a rate of one every 15 minutes.

Mass extinctions have occurred before. But this may be the first time in Earth's history that they were caused on this scale by human irresponsibility. There are now 46 animals on the Kansas Threatened or Endangered Species List. About 75 percent of these are so designated because of habitat loss and pollution. The proposed expansion of Fort Riley by another 100,000 acres of Flint Hills grassland for tank training is an example of such habitat destruction.

The Ogallala Aquifer, the body of underground water reaching from South Dakota to Texas, is being drained by irrigation pumps faster than it is being recharged by rainfall. Federal geologists recently reported that the huge sand dunes underlying much of the Great Plains may easily resurface if global warming weakens the vegetation that now anchors the dunes. This process has already begun in western Texas.

Even the 60-hectare (144-acre) per minute destruction of tropical forests is likely to affect our prairies. Each year an area of tropical forest greater than the size of New York state is lost to human greed. The reduced absorption of carbon dioxide by removed trees and the increased carbon dioxide emission by the burning of forest scraps threatens to increase global temperatures. Actual effects are not known. But weather patterns and ocean currents will certainly change, probably in a direction adverse to human survival and to the prairie in which we live.

Peter Raven, director of the Missouri Botanical Garden, told the Houston assembly of biology teachers that poverty plus the rapid flow of resources from poor to rich countries has led to the most rapid loss of variety among living creatures that the world has seen in 65 million years. And poverty forces further habitat destruction. A mother with hungry children doesn't worry about global warming, tropical forests or species diversity. Already 35,000 children die of starvation each day.

As the human population grows and the wants of each of us increase, we will have to discover a new, resource-rich planet, or adjust our lives to the limits of the planet we now occupy.

A Fossil Hunt

We ate our lunch beside a quiet pool in the Flint Hills about five kilometers east of the Marion-Chase County line. The pool is filled by runoff from occasional rains and a continuous trickle from the crumbling limestone strata exposed on the east bank. A cattle trail led us to the pool through prairie grasses, dried broomweed, fruiting sumac, and buckbrush holding onto its small red berries. It was mid-November and the purples and coppers of the bluestems and switchgrass set the colortone of the grassy hills around. Here and there, the first-year rosettes of flannel mullein added a touch of green to the fall scene.

Middle-aged trees courted the edge of the dry stream bed from the pool further south. And only a half-dozen yellow leaves hung tightly to the cottonwood whose streamside roots were exposed due to the erosive action of the intermittent stream. A sycamore had lost its leaves to the pool where they soaked in various stages of decay.

The rocks below the artesian trickle were coated with the deep green velvet of a moss taking advantage of the damp habitat. And watercress was clinging to the steep incline that leads to the pool. Six school boys threw flint rocks into the pool just to see the water splash. A small unidentified frog sat in the water's edge probably wondering (if frogs can wonder) what all the fuss was about.

The middle school class, Fossil Collection and Interpretation, had spent the morning collecting fossils and rocks in the Flint Hills and were ready for their sack lunches.

The highest strata worked by the class bore flint (chert) chipped by Plains Indians to form projectile points (arrowheads) and tools. Much of the flint was embedded in limestone rock. Deeper strata were of solid limestone with the frequent appearance of the fossils of sea creatures called lamp shells or brachiopods. Brachiopods look much like clams. But clams have right and left valves (half shells) while brachiopods have top and bottom valves. Occasional pelecypod, or clam, fossils were extracted from roadcuts.

Three kilometers east, the deeper Cottonwood Limestone outcropping was topped with loose fragments of sea lilies (crinoids) and sea urchins (echinoids). Sea lilies are flower-like relatives of the starfish. These fragments had probably been released from their stony prison in the Florena Shale by water erosion. The sea urchin fragments were separate plates and a few spines that originally protruded from them.

The surface and much of the internal portion of the Cottonwood Limestone was clearly composed of countless numbers of sea-living fusilinids of the size and shape of wheat grains.

As Todd Becker, Adam Denlinger, Luke Handke, Jared Jost, C.J. Perry, and Tom Watson process the specimens collected, they will be sifting through direct evidence of Kansas' early history.

A. Brachiopod
B. Fusilinids
C. Echinoid spine and plate
D. Crinoid stem

Returning to Marion County, the boys observed the flapping wings of a grounded female northern harrier, formerly called marsh hawk. Thinking it might be injured, the fellows went into the prairie to fetch the bird in distress. But the hawk was dead. The flapping of wings was caused by a brisk south wind.

From an early shallow sea that gave life to myriads of sea creatures, to a grassland that gives life today to a hawk or a frog—that is a sweep of 250 million years. And the human mind can experience this sweep by wandering across the prairie. Or by sitting (or kneeling) on the limestone that crops out along the rim of grassland valleys.

The "Buffalo" Auction

The buffalo burger is tasty in spite of the mist and light rain. The dampened hills here among the headwaters of Gypsum Creek are the site of the annual November buffalo auction at Maxwell Game Refuge in northeast McPherson County. Most of the 118 bison to be sold today are from the state herd at Maxwell; others are trucked in from Garden City and Kingman. And a group of United Methodist Men are selling buffalo burgers to feed the bidders and spectators at the auction.

The 118 American bison up for auction represent surplus animals produced this year, the largest number in the 15-year history of the sale. This is remarkable in the light of the history of the bison population in the U.S.

Bison originated in Asia and migrated to North America across the land bridge connecting Siberia and Alaska during the last ice age. By 1800, they numbered an estimated 60 million. As recently as 1871, a herd of four million bison were reported in southwest Kansas. When the Spanish re-introduced the horse into America, the natives hunted bison more intensely. And the invading Europeans, in an effort to eliminate the natives, deliberately attempted to destroy the bison populations on which they depended for food, shelter, clothing and tools. By the end of the last century, bison numbers were reduced to less than 600. Through the extraordinary efforts of conservationists, preserves were established. Today, there may be as many as 100,000 bison in national parks, preserves and private ranches in North America and abroad. The species is not now in danger of extinction.

The Maxwell herd was begun in 1951 with seven cows and three bulls from the Wichita Mountains (Oklahoma) National Wildlife Refuge. The breeding stock originated in the New York Zoological Park. The 2,254-acre game refuge here will host a remaining herd of 70 individual bison, according to current manager Cliff Peterson.

The relatively small size of today's bison herds require herd managers to periodically purchase new cows or bulls to avoid extensive in-breeding. One buyer here today from Maryland is reported to operate a private bison herd which he markets through his restaurant.

He is here to enlarge his herd and add genetic diversity. Genetic diversity is probably the reason for today's top price of $1,100 for one two-year-old bull.

Bison are attractive range animals for several reasons. They produce meat that is lean and low in cholesterol. They are equipped to digest a much greater variety of prairie grasses and broad-leaved plant species than cattle are. And because they are developed to utilize prairie grasses, bison are said to produce more meat per unit area of range than domestic cattle do.

Among the spectators at today's auction is Glen Davis who managed the Maxwell herd from 1958 to 1974. When told about the unsuccessful attempts to unload six stubborn bison of the 47 trucked in from Garden City, the crusty plainsman remarked that you can chase a buffalo "if you chase him where he wants to go." But each year, he continued, the bison seem to be a little gentler. Davis now raises quarter horses near Canton.

The hills surrounding the bison holding pens, though dripping wet today, still display the splendor of fall colors so characteristic of the tallgrass prairies. The coppers and light purples will probably last until winter. By now, the tall grasses have already transferred their nutrients underground to energize new shoots when higher temperatures return in spring. The warmth and moisture of spring will hasten the final decay of dried leaves and stems of the past season and enrich the soil for which the prairies are known. New growth will be eaten and transformed into myriads of prairie animals, including the majestic American bison.

A Fox in the Night

Emerging from the early morning darkness of the roadside ditch, the red fox approached the roadway between the city shop and U.S. Highway 56. Its long muzzle, pointed ears and bushy deep red tail with a white tip were unmistakable even in the 6:12 a.m. light of December.

Since that 1991 December morning, others have reported similar sightings in this area. Kaye Bartel observed two foxes north of Peabody. Bob Rose, biology teacher at Wichita Collegiate school reported the rearing of a litter of pups by wild foxes in a backyard on East Thirteenth Street in Wichita! Life in urban areas avoids the threat of coyotes.

Red foxes are found over Alaska, most of Canada and much of the eastern half of the U.S. In Kansas, they were originally restricted to the mixed forests, grasslands and rocky hillsides of the eastern third of the state. But they have extended their range westward to cover the entire state.

The red fox feeds mainly on mice and other small mammals, rabbits and other medium-sized mammals, grasshoppers and other insects and fleshy fruits and seeds. Occasional ground-nesting birds, reptiles and amphibians are eaten. Carrion is consumed if relatively fresh.

Red foxes are active mainly at night but they may begin their activity as early as two hours before dark and continue until four hours after sunup. At midday, they return to their den, usually dug into the loose, well-drained soils of hillsides or in heavy brush or woodlands. Dens may have several openings and the tunnels may extend one and a half meters into the ground.

These foxes breed from late December into March. The female then prepares one or more dens and bears an average of five pups. The male provides food for both the pups and the female.

The pups' eyes open at about eight days. The young foxes venture from the den at about four weeks and are weaned at about nine weeks. Before weaning, the pups may be moved to a different den. After 10 weeks, the parents take their pups on hunting trips. By four months, the pups capture their own prey. In autumn, the nearly grown pups leave their parents' home range and live solitary lives until the breeding season. These foxes do not hibernate.

The wily red fox appears to prosper in spite of the human invasion of its habitat and heavy hunting. Its numbers are controlled by diseases such as distemper, rabies, hepatitis and mange.

Kansas mammologist E. Raymond Hall has described the red fox as one of our handsomest mammals; "its bright red color, huge tail with a white tip and graceful carriage make it an unusually attractive creature."

WINTER

The Christmas Bird Count

I am looking forward to the 91st annual Christmas Bird Count. From December 15 (1990) through January 2, over 42,000 participants in 1,500 locations from Canada into South America will count birds.

The counts were begun in 1900 with 27 participants in 25 locations in reaction to a traditional hunting contest on Christmas Day. Choosing sides, hunters competed by shooting anything in sight having feathers or fur. Naturalist Frank M. Chapman wanted to highlight conservation rather than destruction of wildlife. He was also interested in measuring bird populations at the climax of their southern migration. The counts have developed into competitions in which participants try to increase their species count beyond nearby areas or their own previous records.

Each counting area is a circle with a 24-km (15-mile) diameter. Larger groups are divided into smaller parties which are assigned to areas within the circle.

In addition to identifying and counting birds, observers record time and distance spent in various habitats. Observers must be on count for at least eight hours.

The nearest count here is in Harvey County with the center of its circle 9.25 km (5.75 miles) northeast of Halstead and includes the Little Arkansas River, Sand Creek and Sand Prairie Natural History Reservation. Counters meet at 6:45 a.m. and count until 5:30 p.m., with time out for lunch. One need not be a birding expert to participate.

The Harvey County Christmas Bird Count began in 1949 when three young bird watchers walked along Sand Creek with binoculars in hand. They were Bethel College biologist Dwight Platt, one-time Goessel biology teacher Roy Henry, and a current Marion County resident, Jim Rich. Currently, 20 to 25 observers participate, observing 50-60 species collectively. Last year's international high species count was 226 at Freeport, Texas.

Tramping through the prairie, beside wooded streams, or along hedge rows is a pleasant way to get back in touch with your biological roots.

●   ●   ●

This mid-December day turned out to be nearly ideal for the Harvey County Christmas Count. The sun warmed the air from -2° to 8°C. The 0 to 25 km/h wind allowed birds to feed freely. Twenty-four bird watchers registered and were assigned to six small groups.

Biologist Dwight Platt, organizer of the count, was also the leader of our small group. Marilyn Johnson and her daughter Shari were the other members of our team.

Our team spent most of the morning hiking across Sand Prairie Natural History Reservation which is managed by the Bethel College Biology Department. This is an 80-acre plot of mostly stabilized sand dunes near the Harvey County West Park. Due to poor drainage, lowlands are occasionally flooded and provide a variety of habitats for both aquatic and dryland vegetation. Dwight, assisted by Marilyn and other then-students, made a study of the area published in 1973. They identified at least 290 species of vascular plants on the reservation. Most of these plants are dormant now awaiting the "rebirth" of spring. But between thickets of willows and buttonbush are seed-bearing plants that provide sustenance for wintering birds.

Highlights of the morning were the robins, bluebirds and eagles. While a few northern robins usually spend the winter here, the 270 American robins seen at Sand Prairie surprised us. In spring, they will likely move back north and be replaced by others that wintered in Mexico and the Gulf area.

We counted 27 eastern bluebirds. These bright blue thrushes with reddish-brown breasts have made a comeback from their low numbers a few years ago. Both robins and bluebirds feed on the cedar "berries" so plentiful in the Midwest.

We were thrilled by the steady flight of two golden eagles that passed over Sand Prairie.

They were the giants of today's sky.

After lunch, we hiked along the Little Arkansas River and nearby fields for three meandering miles. The dark gray northern juncos were abundant along hedges and brushy fence rows. We saw the brilliant red of male cardinals flitting in the shrubbery. And we counted numerous American goldfinches with their undulating flight and noted their preference for open country with weedy fields and scattered shrubs.

We saw many American tree sparrows, each with a tiny dark spot on its breast, and a red-brown cap. A sharp-skinned hawk made a diving pass at one flock of perching tree sparrows. This hawk has an appetite for small birds.

The wooded edge of the river has its own appeal. The many felled trees reminded us of the violent storms of the summer just past. A white-breasted nuthatch was "climbing down" a tree trunk searching for insects wintering in the bark. And Marilyn observed a male golden-crowned kinglet. This tiny nervous bird with a yellow and orange cap is only one-tenth as tall as an eagle.

By now, our group had identified about 40 species of birds. The collective species count for all groups was 61, second to the record high of 64 in 1986. The individual bird count was a record 31,385. Of that total, an estimated 20,000 American crows were seen at the county landfill along with many European starlings and ring-billed gulls.

Climbing the flood bank of the river to walk the corn field, we passed a small private dumping ground. The heads of two deer, their hides and legs, and an empty rib cage caught our attention. We had seen the perches of bow hunters in the trees. Shari felt a dainty hoof with the toe of her boot.

The sun was low in the western sky when we reached the north road. By now we were eager for a beaten path. The soft sandy soil doesn't make for easy walking. We decided to follow the road for the three-mile hike back to the car.

Within the last two miles of the day, Dwight halted and pointed across Sand Prairie to the southwest. There, silhouetted against the last light of the evening sky, was the stark form of a distant cottonwood. And perched on an upper limb was the unmistakable form of a great horned owl. What a fitting way to close a perfect day! And we could add another name to our bird list.

●　　●　　●

Meteorologists predicted cold, windy weather with possible snow flurries by nightfall for the 1992 December 19 Christmas Bird Count in Harvey County. So why would 24 people choose to spend 9.5 hours in the prairies, fields and woodlands identifying and counting birds?

Of course the bird counts, collectively, generate information on the distribution and population centers of a continent's winter bird life. But there are more personal reasons that motivate most of us.

I look forward to spending the day in a variety of natural and altered landscapes. We will search for goldfinches in sunflower patches and for meadowlarks in grasslands. We expect field sparrows in old fields and shrubby prairies. In the dense brush are rufous-side towhees. A pine siskin may appear in the scattered red cedars. Black-capped chickadees sound their *fee-bee-bee* in woodlands. We observe red-tailed hawks over fields and fence rows. Harris sparrows flock in shelterbelts and hedges. Blue jays scream along wooded creek banks. A mockingbird flies into a roadside thicket. Song sparrows frequent brush and marshlands along with tree sparrows. Horned larks and Lapland longspurs hide in the stubble of open fields. We see yellow-bellied woodpeckers clinging to upright limbs in the woodland. And rock doves (pigeons) cluster on farmsteads. We saw all of these on this "cold, windy" day.

Another special satisfaction I experience on bird counts is seeing birds I don't usually see. The variety of habitats visited increases the opportunity to see many species. This year, our team alone recorded 34 species; the total for all our teams was 63. Many of these are common. But I seldom see the spectacular blue of the eastern bluebirds we saw this year. We watched a yellow-rumped warbler flit from branch to branch in a prairie shrub. In 1970, we observed a Townsend's solitaire perched near the peak of a coniferous tree in a cemetery. The house finch, now becoming more common, was absent or rare here until recent years. And the majestic golden eagles in flight over Sand Prairie several winters ago provide a lasting memory.

A day of combing the countryside for birds also provides an informal opportunity to survey the quality of wildlife habitat in terms of protective cover and food supply. Have plants produced ample fruits and seeds for the winter ahead? Do custodians of the land consider the needs of the wildlife with whom we share this planet?

Another personal bonus from the count is to be with people who know more about birds than I do and who are willing to share what they know. The range of knowledge and skills among participants varies from those of long-time bird watchers who have participated in this count for most of its 44 years, to novices who have paid little serious attention to birds until the day of this count. In our team of four, Al, a biology teacher, was here on his first count. Al's son, Jason, is a middle-school student. Carolyn, our team leader, is a nurse and a seasoned bird watcher. Al and Carolyn served as mentors sharing binoculars with Jason and pointing out distinguishing features in a bird's color patterns, shape and behavior. Books were used if verbal descriptions were inadequate. Carolyn compliments Jason's alertness in spotting a great horned owl in flight.

The camaraderie one experiences with fellow birders is another benefit of the bird count. Whether student, chemist, farmer, city official, taxidermist, artist, homemaker, wildlife specialist, psychologist, grocer, philosopher, biologist or psychiatrist, all share a common interest in feathered creatures. Gathering at noon to eat the lunches we bring in paper bags, all teams compare notes on observations made so far. During the afternoon hours, we concentrate on those habitats most likely to reveal the species not yet seen. It is a team effort. And we all want to spot every species present in our 177 square-mile observation area.

An added benefit of a day of bird counting is the surprises we meet in addition to bird sightings. Dead on the road was what appeared to be a badger. Al turned over many rocks and logs, calling our attention to interesting insect larvae, snails and slugs. Rocks and logs were returned to original positions.

An ornate box turtle not yet settled in for the winter raised questions. It looked fresh except for its slightly sunken eyes. Al and Jason took it home for recuperation but it never recovered.

While I was concentrating on a flock of chickadees, the others saw three white-tailed deer cross the clearing behind me. Although I missed the sighting, the apparent pleasure it provided the team helped make this bird count another satisfying experience.

Tumbleweeds

We sprayed the tumbleweed with white paint and sprinkled it with glitter. That was the Christmas "tree" for our biology classroom at Radium Rural High School in central Kansas during the mid-1950s. Christmas can be celebrated without spruce and fir.

Our tumbleweed of choice, common in the area, was the Russian thistle, described as a great wanderer and known by botanists as *Salsola iberica*.

The Russian thistle has several forms. The globelike form may be over a meter wide providing prickly summer shelters for rabbits, mice, and birds. "Then," says ecologist David Costello, "when the roaring winds of autumn pluck them from their moorings, they become swift-moving balls that race across the landscape," and pile up against shrubs and fences. A wind shift then sees them rolling off in another direction. Some of its 20,000 seeds are attached loosely, others are buried next to its stems. So as the tumbleweed rolls, every bare area in its path is sprinkled with seeds during its several months of travel. Even those seeds that never let go may sprout when covered with drifting soil.

The Russian thistle was introduced into South Dakota in about 1873 from Russia where it was a serious weed. The Russians called it *perekati-pole*, meaning "roll-across-the-field." Brought in with flax seed, it quickly spread over the western half of the United States to occupy cultivated fields, roadsides, railroads, and other disturbed sites.

This wanderer is one of the first plants to appear during drought. In early spring, it is grazed by livestock and can be cut for hay. It can be prepared and served on our tables like spinach. And its greenish flowers develop tiny black seeds which can be ground into meal.

But on mature plants, the two- to eight-centimeter, fleshy, spine-tipped leaves render them inedible for man or beast. Cattlemen know that these plants occasionally accumulate nitrates and oxalates in toxic concentrations.

The name tumbleweed also applies to several other species, one also in the Goosefoot Family, another a pigweed. Even cafes, bars, and motels claim the name "Tumbleweed." And the detached plant is seen rolling across the plains in hundreds of old Western movies.

Tumbleweeds have inspired at least one western tune made popular by the Sons of the Pioneers. Bob Nolan, who wrote the words and music to *Tumbling Tumbleweeds*, depicts a cowboy riding "underneath a prairie moon." "Lonely but free I'll be found drifting along with the tumbling tumbleweeds" hardly inspires responsible living. But "cares of the past are behind," and "a new world's born at dawn" suggest the therapeutic value of periodic relaxation to avoid the burnout of over-commitment. And the daily renewal of hope and new beginnings.

Maybe we can all learn from the tumbleweed.

The Dugout at Cub Creek

Standing out from the south bank of the flood plain was the front wall of a dug-out carved back into the slope. A second dugout, just meters east of the first, housed a flock of chickens. Closer to the creek, a pole frame held up a roof and three walls composed of corn stalks that provided minimal protection for a single horse and a goat.

The first dugout was the dwelling of Herman Schmale who lived among the bur oaks and American elms that lined Cub Creek. He eked out his living raising Leghorn chickens—sometimes as many as 300. During daytime hours, the chickens ranged freely among the trees. Herman took his eggs to market periodically with his horse and buggy and returned with a few groceries.

Herman's goat provided milk for his supper. His horse pulled the walking plow to prepare the small bottomland field for planting corn and various garden crops. Brother Ted remembers seeing rows of corn among the scattered tree stumps. In a good year, the corn reached a height of four to five meters (12-15 ft). Herman controlled weeds with a hoe.

For meat, Herman hunted small game. On a cold winter day, one might see the carcass of a rabbit hanging from a tree limb or there might be a muskrat ready to be skinned. Fallen limbs and dead trees along the creek provided fuel. He had dug a well with a post-hole auger but later tapped spring water by driving a pipe into the bank of Cub Creek.

Herman Schmale lived his simple life up-creek from my grandparent's farm over in Nebraska's Jefferson County. When visiting our grandparents, my brothers, cousins and I often headed into the woods to see Mr. Schmale.

On rare occasions, we entered his dug-out. It was square, about five meters (15 ft) on a side. I remember the smell of damp soil and wood smoke. At the center of the cave, two 55-gallon drums lay on their sides, end-to-end, to serve as space heater and cook stove. They were flattened a bit to keep the cooking pot and frying pan from sliding down to the dirt floor. A series of stove pipes led most, but not all, of the wood smoke to the outdoors. The aroma was pleasant but the leaked smoke stung our eyes.

Herman's brass bed stood on the ground near the east dirt wall. Brother Richard remembers a shotgun hanging against the wall and an old clock. I wondered what difference the time of day meant to him. Perhaps the clock was a relic reminding him of his more affluent past.

According to Uncle Ernest, Herman had come to these prairies from Germany at the age of about 15 years. In the early 1930s, he invested heavily in purebred hogs, a venture that proved unsuccessful. He lost most of his possessions. In about 1932, he moved to this nine-acre patch along the creek. Here, among bur oaks, screaming blue jays and raucous crows, Herman lived his quiet life.

Compared to the thousands of homeless people in the world, Herman was rich. He had all the space, food, water and shelter he really needed. While occasional flooding destroyed some of his flock, and raccoons nibbled on his corn, he always had enough left to survive.

With an expanding human population and shrinking resources, we may all need to tighten our belts and rediscover the real world. We add luxuries to our lives and pass them on to our children as necessities. Our children, in turn do the same. So the line that distinguishes needs from wants becomes blurred. Herman Schmale helps clarify that line for me.

We have a way of becoming possessed by our possessions. How much of our work pays for necessities? How much for possessions? How much for military protection of our possessions? How much for pleasure?

In recent years, Herman Schmale's sister suggested to Aunt Marie that the family was somewhat humiliated by his lifestyle. But I have a hunch that there was something wholesome about living as a companion to wild creatures. In the book, *Kansas Wildlife*, Joseph T. Collins observes that even a glimpse of the wilderness restores "our sense of balance in a people-oriented world."

Almost Snowbound

Whether from a swirling blizzard or a silent settling of flakes, the white blanket that covers the prairie always brings rich childhood memories of Nebraska winters. To awaken to a "universe of sky and snow" seemed always to lead to unexpected adventure.

Walking to school took extra effort as each step pushed against a mountain of snow. But the reward of sledding down the slope at Lonesome Ridge School made it worthwhile. About half the school ground was flat like the fields to the south and east. Then an abrupt slope dropped sharply to the northwest and leveled off toward the creek. A blanket of nearly melting snow made for perfect sledding.

A single established sledding path cleared through the hillside shrubs, descended toward a green ash tree, curved to avoid it and continued on to the north fence. That course was not without hazard. My schoolmate Lawrence once missed the turn and broke an arm bone against that tree. The accident may have prompted the change to a bluff in Henry von Steen's nearby pasture. Here the slope was steeper, but the north fence no longer posed a barrier, and there was no ash tree to fret our teacher. With boughten sleds, we could glide almost to the creek.

In addition to the boughten sleds, there was the homemade sled that Dad built, and the inverted top of an abandoned organ stool. The stool put the seat of its passenger right next to the melting snow. So, following recess, we studied and recited, standing with our backs to the stove, hoping to dry the seats of our pants before the next recess. The stove stationed at the center of our single classroom served as an efficient public clothes dryer as long as our school's enrollment was only eight or ten.

Walking to school was most trying when the surface snow began melting during the day and then froze into an icy crust that night. On one such occasion, we decided to cross the fields to school. With each step, the icy layer almost supported our weight. But the final shifting of the body for the next step caused the supporting foot to break through. What a walk!

One Saturday, a previous surface thaw and sharp freeze created a perfect crust for ice skating. On our skates, we spent the day gliding effortlessly down hills until occasional break-throughs suggested greater caution. While cold, the day was also sunny. This was the only time we got sunburned in mid-winter.

The deeper snows made travelling difficult. My favorite Christmas Eve trip to our grandparents' farm was the one threatened by heavy snowfall and massive drifting. Even chain lugs on our car's rear wheels wouldn't get us through those drifts. So we drove to a meeting point and rode Uncle Ben's horse-drawn wagon the last several miles to reach our family celebration. The wagon was full of aunts, uncles and cousins keeping each other warm. The horses' hooves and wagon wheels crunched merrily through the snow that dark night. All this added to the excitement of that Christmas Eve.

The deeper snows also covered the food supplies of wildlife. Neighbor Jess Higgins, who owned land on three sides of our seven-acre farmstead, allowed us to explore his pasture at will. When I was 15, a heavy snow prompted brother Ted and me to load small sacks of grain onto our back-racks to supply local wintering birds with accessible food. We plowed through snow past Robbers' Cave and across the creek to the half-mile fence along an Osage orange hedge to reach our feeding station. Later, diminishing food stock and the many birds' tracks provided evidence of the need.

Among the factors that bred caution into our celebrative reception of snowstorms were the tales of the Blizzard of 1888. For a snowstorm to qualify as a blizzard, the temperature drops to -7°C (20°F) and wind speeds reach 56 km/h (35 mi/h). In that Nebraska storm, an uncle of Dad's friend froze to death, having gotten lost in the swirling snow. Even though it happened a year before Dad was born, we knew that "it could happen here."

When heavy snowfall occurred during the school day, I always wished that we would become snowbound. What an adventure that would be! The coal shed was near the school house. And if that fuel supply diminished, the school desks could go. We had no electricity, telephone or lamps, so the nights might be long and dark and mysterious. But we could tell stories and sing songs until the familiar wind whistling past the windows would lull us to sleep. With John Greenleaf Whittier, I thought, "what matter how the night behaved? What matter how the north wind raved? Blow high, blow low, not all its snow could quench our hearth-fires' ruddy glow."

But alas, those fantasies were always dashed by a horse-drawn wagon appearing through the confusion of snowflakes before nightfall. Always a concerned father would rescue us prematurely from being "shut in from all the world about."

So we were deprived of the experience that Whittier described poetically in "Snowbound."

A Stone Fence in Winter

It was a bright January Sunday afternoon in the Flint Hills. Friday's snow had sifted through the grass canopy and rested lightly on the prairie litter. I followed the stone fence that begins seven miles east of the Marion-Chase County line. The fence reaches from Highway 150 a half-mile south into the prairie and then east for about a quarter mile.

This fence of stones is 30 to 40 cm wide and now varies from nearly chin height down to knee level where stones have toppled.

Most of its stones are flat; a few are nearly cubical. All are chunks of the Cottonwood Limestone deposited on the bottom of the shallow sea that existed here about 250 million years ago. Many exhibit fossils of sea creatures on their surface—fusilinids and brachiopods. One stone holds a crinoid stem, part of an ocean creature related to the starfish. Now the dried fruiting stalk of a wild indigo reaches out from between the rocks reminding us that what was sea is now prairie.

Following along the stone fence on each side is a narrow cattle trail now filled with snow. Rabbit tracks dot the trail where cattle have worn down stiff stalks and entangling grasses that would impede a running rabbit.

Fecal pellets near the fence indicate the recent presence of animals not now in sight. Most are those of eastern cottontails. Trampled snow under a thistle suggests that it was an object of attention. Did a small animal pluck thistle down to finish out or repair a nest within the stone fence?

Here and there, a space between adjacent rocks suggests an entrance to a sheltered den. Tracks lead to one such hole with a rabbit-size opening. I mark the location by dragging my foot through the snow. My return trip on the other side reveals a similar opening with rabbit tracks and a few fecal pellets. Apparently the opening is used by rabbits to cross from one segment of the prairie to the other.

Another set of tracks leads to a dried broomweed where the rabbit had paused, dawdled a bit and then moved on.

Here and there are pairs of much smaller tracks, the tracks of each pair side-by-side. Was it a bird that hops, or a mouse that jumps? The afternoon sun has begun melting the snow, making identification difficult.

By now, the snow on some of the stones has disappeared leaving puddles of water that drips down to rocks below.

The yellow-green blotches on the stones are lichens, combinations of algae and fungi. The alga manufactures food from water and carbon dioxide to use it as a source of energy. The fungus, in return for a portion of the food, provides the alga with a protective environment. This lichen not only converts the sun's energy into food energy but it also begins to dissolve rock, converting it into soil.

No mammals or small birds are seen near the stone fence today. The red-tailed hawks and the northern harriers patrolling the prairie skies farther west make this a good time to hide among the stones. And any lizards and snakes would be hidden under the bottom rocks.

Steel stakes now stand along the stone fence row holding three strands of modern barbed wire in place. They compensate for the low spots in the stone fence but provide little shelter from weather and predators that stone fences provide for prairie creatures.

Before leaving the fence, I think back to its builders and to the musings of biologist John Breukelman:

A lovely Sunday drive;
    Restful it should have been
But that my mind would not
    Forget those tired men
Who placed flat stone on stone
    To make a measured pile

So high, so wide, so long,
    Mile after weary mile;
So I arrived at home
    With aching back and arms—
Just seeing those stone fences
    Surrounding Flint Hills farms.

Mammals Survive the Winter

Toward evening, we watched an eastern cottontail munching on twigs or buds just partially covered with snow. As it brushed the snow off its supper, I wondered about my ability to survive the prairie winter had I been dropped, unnoticed, from the last westbound covered wagon of the season.

Fortunately, most prairie creatures are better adapted for winter's icy blasts than I am. Mammals require high body temperature to maintain their active way of life. They do this by producing lots of heat and regulating its loss. Most mammals have layers of fat and a covering of fur that insulates the inside of the body from the cold winter air outside. And when the temperature drops, the brain causes shivering and a decrease of blood flow to the skin.

These mechanisms seem adequate in keeping the cottontail active all winter. This rabbit doesn't even begin the season with excess fat. That would add weight and reduce its speed and agility, increasing its chance of becoming a meal for a coyote or some other predator. So, cottontails eat all winter. They may, however, remain in holes covered with snow up to two days after heavy snowfall.

Striped skunks, on the other hand, spend most cold days in their underground dens located along fence rows or under rock outcrops.

They have fattened up in fall and live on accumulated fat on days that keep them indoors.

Western harvest mice build on or above-ground nests of grasses and other fibrous plants and line them with soft materials such as thistle down. Groups of mice spend cold periods huddled in communal nests.

Fox squirrels may survive snow and ice storms in leaf nests tucked in the crotches of trees. But they prefer nesting in hollow trees with small openings. After heavy snows, they resume their active lives. The walnuts near our house decrease in numbers throughout the winter and piles of discarded hedge apple fibers are evidence of their activity.

The plains pocket gopher spends the winter in its underground nesting chamber, generally below frost line. Convenient tunnels lead to food storage and rest room areas.

The familiar thirteen-lined ground squirrel fattens on seeds and insects and stores extra groceries in its den below frost line. In October or November it plugs the entrance, curls up in its nest, and begins hibernation. Its body temperature drops to meet that of its nest. Breathing motion is reduced from 150 per minute to three or four. And the heart slows from 200-300 beats per minute to 15. Every two or three weeks the squirrel awakens briefly to urinate. One third to one half its body weight is lost before it resumes springtime activity in March or April.

Other Kansas hibernators include several other ground squirrels, the woodchuck, the meadow jumping mouse and several species of bats that inhabit caves or buildings.

There are moments when human hibernation would be a tempting alternative to cold weather and to the business of civilization. But hibernators miss the excitement and challenges of nature that await the alert mind.

Birds in Winter

Nine starlings huddled on the screen covering our neighbor's chimney. It was a cold morning and the birds took advantage of the hot air seeping from the furnace.

Like mammals, birds are warm-blooded. That is, they maintain a fairly constant body temperature even when the environment does not. To maintain that temperature requires the rapid oxidation (burning) of food. Small animals have a high surface area-to-volume ratio and that allows heat to escape. So most birds, being small, must generate more heat than most mammals do. Most of their foods are energy-rich: seeds, fruits, nectar, insects, fish and rodents. And the concentration of sugar in their blood is about double that of human blood. If birds can find food, they can usually handle the cold.

Birds conserve heat by reducing projections from their bodies such as the ears or fleshy tails found in mammals. These projections have a high surface area-to-volume ratio and allow heat loss.

Birds are covered with a lifeless layer of insulating feathers. Observers of fasting pigeons in a -40°C (also -40°F) environment reported that most birds survived for 72 hours. Pigeons that had lost their feathers survived less than a half hour.

Some birds huddle together at night. Fasting starlings roosting separately at a bit below freezing consumed 92 percent more oxygen per bird than when huddled in a group of four. Heat loss from non-feathered legs can be reduced 50 percent by crouching. And a bird can reduce heat loss another 12 percent by tucking its head into its shoulder feathers. Some birds even dive into deep snow to survive especially cold periods.

In spite of these physical adaptations, many birds that nest in Kansas migrate south for the winter. Traveling to southern states are cowbirds, red-wings, field sparrows and turkey vultures. The house wren travels to the Gulf states or into Mexico. Brown thrashers, hummingbirds and mourning doves fly to southern states or as far as Panama. Dickcissels and Baltimore orioles move to Central and South America. Martin house residents winter in Brazil. As a boy in Nebraska, I could go barefooted when the barn swallows returned to our barn from Mexico and Brazil. And the great blue herons that nest in Kansas sycamore trees usually spend the winter in southern states or in South America.

As mammals, we lack wings for migration and as humans, we lack enough body hair for warmth. So in a culture that frowns on obesity, we must either burrow into the ground, or build a fire, or dig out our heavy underwear to survive the prairie winter.

Cold-Blooded Animals in Winter

Live boxelder bugs in mid winter? We see them on warm days that sometimes sneak into this otherwise cold season. How do they survive cold days? Mammals and birds generate lots of heat and regulate its loss. But what about those prairie creatures that can't generate the amount of heat used by birds and mammals?

Like some birds, monarch butterflies fly to southern states or to Central America to return in spring. But most insects spend the winter right here in some state of dormancy either as adults, nymphs, pupae, larvae or eggs. Adult boxelder bugs, wasps, houseflies, many beetles and some butterflies find protected places in which they survive the winter. Occasionally, they emerge to bask in the sun on unseasonably warm days. Most dragonflies, damselflies, mayflies and dobsonflies winter as immature nymphs. And, of course, cicada nymphs may spend several years underground sucking juices from plants before they emerge. Many moths and butterflies spend the winter in cocoons. The larval state is the winter "choice" of June beetles and woolybears. And adult praying mantises, grasshoppers and crickets die in fall relying on their eggs to continue their species next season.

Among the relatives of insects are the nearly-microscopic waterfleas, commonly eaten by small fish. During most of the year, waterfleas produce eggs that do not require fertilization. These eggs produce females which produce more eggs of that same kind. This process continues until conditions become less favorable. During drought, cold weather or failure in food supply, some of the eggs develop into males. Other eggs are of such nature that they require fertilization. The eggs that are fertilized by males lie dormant, often withstanding extremes of dry or cold weather, until conditions become more favorable. This dormancy may last for months or even years.

Wintering earthworms plug the openings to their burrows and descend to below frost line. Here they await spring either alone or rolled up with several worms.

Fish, frogs, lizards, turtles and snakes, like insects, waterfleas and worms, are also "coldblooded." That means that their body temperatures tend to follow that of their surroundings, so they need less food and oxygen when they are cold. As kids, we once thawed a fish from a layer of solid ice removed from the creek. It had survived its icy trap and swam on its way.

Most of our lizards, land turtles, toads and snakes retreat into the ground for the winter. Some find refuge in the burrows and dens of other animals. Most of our frogs and aquatic turtles burrow into the bottom mud of ponds and streams. In eastern Kansas, many snakes and lizards winter beneath large rocks or in the crevices of rocky hillsides.

Plants have their own ways of coping with winter. Our annuals spend the cold season as dormant seeds. Tall prairie grasses channel nutrients from their leaves into underground storage tissue for the winter. And broad-leaved trees drop their leaves for the cold, dry seasons so they lose little moisture by evaporation and use little water in food-making.

In the Midwest, frequent and drastic changes in temperatures are not uncommon and the animals and plants that have appropriate means of adaptation are the ones that make up the communities of the prairie.

Weasels, Armadillos, and Musk Thistles

Clara Bartel was startled by the sudden appearance of a white mouse-sized creature in her bathroom doorway. It was a cold morning in 1987 and Clara was getting dressed for worship services at her church. The animal's aggressive posture dared her to invade his territory! Clara called a neighbor to the rescue. He killed the creature and tossed it out into the alley.

Two weeks later, Clara telephoned to relate her discovery, suggesting my possible interest. The frozen body, about as long as a pencil (16 cm), was still intact in the back alley, having somehow avoided the jaws of neighborhood cats. Perhaps it was its frozen condition, or the odor emitted by the anal glands of this species. For what had "threatened" Clara was a least weasel.

Least weasels commonly live in grasslands where they eat various field mice with occasional birds and insects. They require up to half their body weight in food each day. To meet this requirement, they thrust their long slender bodies into the runways and dens of their underground prey. Their own nests are usually built in the abandoned burrows of mice, gophers or moles.

The summer coat of this small weasel is brown with white undersides. But Clara's weasel was dressed in its all-white winter pelage.

The first verified capture of a least weasel in Kansas was in March 1964 near Marysville in Marshall County. Since then they have been seen in several additional northern counties.

Tabor College biologists Max Terman and Virleen Bailey reported sightings of these small mammals in Marion and Harvey Counties by 1985. The species appears to be expanding its range southward.

Several summers ago, a nine-banded armadillo was nose-plowing its way through litter on the forest floor near Armand Bayou in southeast Texas. Son-in-law Tony and I watched as it foraged for insects, worms and occasional berries, apparently unaware of our presence. All other armadillos I had ever seen were road-kills observed on rare trips into Oklahoma and Texas.

On June 6, 1990, elementary teacher Evan Yoder reported the road-kill of an armadillo near his farm at Peabody. So far, armadillos are uncommon in Kansas but are reported to be extending their range northward.

In 1932 the musk thistle was reported in Kansas only in Washington County at the Nebraska border. In 1948 it was still described as rare in Kansas. The first musk thistle I ever noticed was in Dickinson County in 1960. In 1963 a musk thistle displayed its handsome, nodding head about a mile east of Lost Springs in Marion County. By 1976, it was found in most counties of the eastern two-thirds of the state. This intensely competitive species is clearly extending its range southward across the prairie.

The prairie has always been an arena of change. Some creatures expand their range and others disappear. The last verified sighting of the black-footed ferret in Kansas occurred in 1957. It was once found in mixed and short grass prairie regions of the western two-thirds of the state.

Some population changes were prompted by grand geologic upheavals like the uplift of the Rocky Mountains. A related factor was variation in climate. But population pressures on prairie creatures are increasingly determined by human activity. Even the way we farm affects the habitat of prairie creatures. A meadowlark isn't likely to complete its reproductive duties on a farm without sizable, undisturbed fence rows or meadows. A redwing will search for another nesting site if we drain its marsh.

But why should we care about meadowlarks or redwings? In mining country, test canaries were lowered into shaft mines to test the air for safety. If the canary died, the miners knew that the mine was unsafe for them, too.

Why should we care about the extinction of a fish or a small snail? We might as well ask why we should care about the death of a miner's canary.

Tracking Rabbits

On this last day of February, barking dogs and shotgun blasts occasionally interrupt my afternoon hike through the fields and woodlands along French Creek. Overhead, occasional flocks of Canada geese head north and then west. Between patches of snow, melt-water saturates the ground and litter, supplying moisture to the myriads of green leaves already emerging from their wintry tomb.

Here at the edge of a rock pile is the den of an eastern woodrat. It would be interesting to dismantle the brush pile nest to inspect its various chambers, but it could already be sheltering a litter of young ones. Later, I observe another den at the crown of a felled tree.

Standing up from the snow are seed-bearing Illinois bundleflower and roundhead lespedeza. The deep-red berries of buckbrush abound but appear not to be a popular wildlife food. Nearby milo fields still provide grain to turkeys, pheasants, quail and ducks. On state-controlled lands, wildlife officials require one-third of the crop to remain unharvested. And the unusually wet fall and winter have kept farmers from completing their milo harvest. So, many birds and mammals along French Creek have plenty of food this winter.

In the patches of melting snow, the tracks of eastern cottontail and wild turkey are easily recognized. But because of widespread melting, tracking these creatures is impossible today. Before melting, tracking can be a game.

Ernest Thompson Seton, in a book first published in 1912, described his adventures in tracking wild animals. Plying his trade as naturalist, he follows the tracks of an animal and describes its activities as interpreted from his knowledge of natural history.

In February of 1902, this early leader in the Boy Scout movement found himself in a hotel in Newton, Kansas. In the hotel office, he asked his usual question, "Any wild animals about here?" He got the usual answer, "No, all been shot off." Walking down the street about four blocks, he found a jackrabbit's trail in the snow.

Both cottontails and jackrabbits place their hind feet ahead of their front feet tracks. Seton knew this was a jackrabbit's trail because its larger hind feet landed one a little farther forward than the other. In cottontails, the hind feet land beside each other. Jacks also leave a streak in the snow with their long hanging tail. And while cottontails cover one to two meters (three to seven ft) in each bound, this rabbit bounded 3.5 to 4.5 m (12 to 15 ft) when not pressed by predators.

While still in town, Seton saw cottontail tracks. A mile into the country, he met an old farmer who insisted "No rabbits were ever found around here." A quarter mile further on was a fenced orchard. Snow drifts half buried the fence and filled the spaces among the stalks of tall prairie grasses. At the edge of the drift, he found the den of a jackrabbit, no doubt a black-tailed jackrabbit. The only tracks visible were leading away from the den suggesting that the rabbit had entered the den before last night's snow.

Seton followed the tracks. An experienced jackrabbit when pressed, says Seton, "runs with long, low hops, from six to seven in succession, then gives an upright leap to make an observation." This jackrabbit was making observation leaps only once in 12 hops. Then he must have encountered a dog for he stretched to six-meter (20 ft) leaps.

When Seton finally saw the jackrabbit, it was sitting under a barbed wire fence looking back at him. The rabbit had led Seton and other pursuers through fences, hedges and barnyards, never letting him approach within 180 m (200 yards). After more than three kilometers (two miles) of tracking, Seton was brought back to his starting point near the orchard.

Seton concluded that this was indeed a very clever rabbit. He had used an effective obstacle course to avoid capture. And he "could live and flourish on the edge of a town that was swarming with dogs and traveled over daily by men with guns."

Bison in Winter

The rising sun pushed up to join the ring of clouds hovering over the horizon. On the day that is to become the east coast's winter "storm of the century," most of the snow here at the Maxwell Game Refuge has melted. Last season's grass cover forms a tangle of yellow, dull-orange and brown stalks over the rounded hills. These colors and the deep gray of the timber along the creeks and the patches of wild plum and sumac in the grasslands dominate the March 13 landscape. The soil here is sandy; on a distant hillside is a patch of bare sand.

Cliff Peterson, refuge manager, drives his pickup truck with a load of protein pellets meant to supplement the grass diet of bison and elk. Big bluestem and other tall prairie grasses transfer enough nutrients from their leaves and stems into their roots for the winter that bison and elk benefit from this mixture of grains and alfalfa. Some range ecologists think that bison originally migrated westward for winters because the shorter prairie grasses there do not withdraw the nutrients from their winter leaves.

"We usually feed the bison first," says Cliff, "otherwise they chase the elk away." But today we find the elk first, out of the sight of bison. Actually it is the elk that find us. The sight of the truck attracts 10 bull elk. One has already lost an antler. The others will lose theirs soon, only to grow another pair during the summer.

As Cliff activates a switch, the pellets are flipped to the ground forming a trail behind us. The elk define that trail as they locate the pellets.

The term "elk," by the way, is used by Europeans to refer to what Americans call "moose." So zoologists prefer the name "wapiti," a Shawnee Indian word meaning "pale rump," in reference to the large yellowish patch in the tail area of these antlered creatures.

Over the next hill, the bison approach. Some cross ahead of us, and Cliff weaves the pickup this way and that to avoid hitting the huge mammals. He remembers how a cow once pushed another against his pickup, denting its side. The 150 bison form a long wavy line behind the pickup, tracing the trail we have just made with pellets.

Scattering the pellets over the hills, Cliff explains, avoids the congestion of grazers and the consequent trampling of prairie grasses. Such trampling would expose the sandy soil here to wind erosion.

"What would happen to these animals if you wouldn't provide the supplement?" I asked.

Most of the animals would survive, he said, but we might lose two or three more head of the older animals over the winter.

This winter has not been severe enough to be a problem for these well-adapted critters. Bison challenge the winter winds by facing directly into them. It is the front of these animals, after all, that has the longer hair. When the snow is deep, the bison pushes its snout into the snow and sweeps its head from side to side exposing the grasses beneath for grazing.

In winter, cows and calves graze together while bulls form a protective circle around them. In earlier times, gray wolves followed the roving herds and waited for calves or aged animals to become separated from the herd. In deep snow, even bulls were attacked by severing the tendons of their hind legs, and then tearing at their flanks, weakening the victims by loss of blood. Grizzly bears also preyed on bison.

We drive another mile and a half on west to feed the remaining 40 wapiti. Their herding behavior is especially strong in winter. Here, a number of cows, a few adult bulls, and several yearling bulls came for pellets. The yearling bulls have small spikes contrasting with the majestic antlers of the older bulls. The cows do not have antlers.

In late spring, this herd of wapiti will break up for birthing, the cows forming smaller groups which may include a few immature males.

The two large mammals here at Maxwell call attention to the difference between antlers and horns. Male members of the deer family develop antlers of solid bone growing from the skull. They are shed each year and quickly regrown. Horns are hollow sheaths capping a bony structure and develop on both sexes of bison, pronghorns, sheep, goats, and cattle. The sheaths are composed of a protein like that of fingernails and hair. They are not shed except in pronghorns.

The feeding done, we stop and chat near the observation tower. Cliff is a 1980 graduate of Kansas State University with a degree in wildlife biology. His training supplements his farm background in managing the herds on this refuge. He dreams of developing an educational visitor's center on this hill and adding a naturalist to the staff. The oil wells on the refuge and the annual auctioning of excess bison through the years have certainly provided a sizable income for the Kansas Wildlife and Parks Department. He would like to see it invested here at Maxwell.

SPRING

Red Cedars, Apples, and Rust

Following a recent early April rain, red cedars in our area burst into "bloom." This orange "bloom" really had nothing to do with reproduction of the cedar. But it had everything to do with the reproduction of a common rust fungus that infests the twigs of the eastern red cedar.

The life cycle of this fungus is so complex that it took years to understand it. It was finally discovered that this parasitic species alternates between two hosts—the cedar and the apple. Its spores are carried by winds into the cedar's branches in fall where they spend the winter in its twigs as small gray galls. The gall swells during warm rainy nights to nearly the size of a golf ball. This now-orange sphere explodes to produce many jelly-like tentacles which produce spores. The tentacles soon dry and its spores are air-borne and distributed over the countryside. Those alighting on apple trees are ready to resume their life cycles.

The spores now develop into a different form which digests and absorbs nutrients from the tissues of apple leaves and fruits. This infestation damages leaf tissue in spotted areas and reduces the leaves' food-making ability. It also causes spotting of fruits and stunts their growth.

In fall this rust fungus develops a different kind of spore which prairie winds distribute to red cedars as far as several kilometers away. As winter approaches, apple trees lose their leaves and fruits and the apple phase of the rust loses its source of nutrition. But its spores have already found a home in the cedar which retains its scaley leaves through the winter, supplying food for both itself and the rust fungus. Thus the species is saved from extinction.

While this winter infection rarely jeopardizes the health of the red cedar, the summer infection can severely damage the apple tree. The good news for the apple tree is that certain varieties of eastern red cedar resistant to the fungus are now available. If these varieties become common, the life cycle of the fungus would be interrupted.

Meanwhile, warm spring rains will continue to usher in the sight of bright orange galls against the cedar's dark foliage. And the cedar-apple rust will continue its cycle.

As wildlife photographer Mike Blair puts it, this fungus is "yet another example of Nature's pathways to efficient perpetuation of life."

Spring in the Sand Hills

In mid-April, the sand hills are covered with a mix of last season's prairie grasses, the awakening woody plants and new green growth on the sandy floor. Chickasaw plums are blooming and bearing new leaves. New foliage is also emerging from other perennials: prairie rose, aromatic sumac and black locust. The bayonet leaves of yucca have survived the winter and patches of coralberry are "coming to life," even though last year's berries still cling to its branches. Along the trail, a narrowleaf gromwell extends its cheery yellow blossoms, slender tubes with ruffled, laid-out edges.

I had stopped for a brief look at Sand Hills State Park near Hutchinson. This 468-hectare (1,123-acre) plot was set aside to preserve its sand dunes, grasslands, wet-lands and woodlands. Historically, the sands and gravels eroded from the Rocky Mountains and were washed to this area by the Arkansas River. Prevailing southwesterly winds blew the fine sand from the river valley to the park, forming a band of sand dunes reaching from near Burrton, past Hutchinson and into Rice County. The dune 100 meters ahead is about 13 meters high. Winds have shifted the sands until plants finally stabilized the dune, providing a rich diversity of habitats.

From atop the dune, I see the misty, yellow-green cottonwoods and willows in the lowland as they begin to generate new foliage. On another dune to the northwest is the pink-purplish splash of a redbud tree in full bloom. At the base of the dune, clusters of greening buttonbush and roughleaf dogwood are already taking advantage of last night's rain.

The glimpse of a brilliant cardinal and the joyous call of a brown thrasher stretch my "brief look" into a several-hour hike.

The prickly pear cactus challenges all oncomers with its spines. A few hairy gromwells are blooming in the path, their flowers more orange-yellow than their cousins seen earlier. Between cracks in the foot bridge, poison ivy shoots begin to emerge. The ground-level leaves of purple poppy mallow are everywhere. And so are new grasses, sedges, white sage and the densely fuzzy leaves of flannel mullein. Several blooming corydalis add yet more yellow to the prairie floor.

Animals are not as obvious here as plants. But the elevated ridges of soil crossing the trail remind us that eastern moles have recently dug their surface tunnels, searching for soil animals. Fresh ant hills, a deer track and the cheery song of a house wren are further signs of animal life. The overhead flight of mourning doves and the frequent glimpses of red admiral butterflies add variety to the afternoon trek.

A few monarch butterflies have returned from their winter home awaiting a new milkweed crop for feeding and egg laying. A few of last year's stalks are still standing. And in the grove of black locusts, silver-spotted skippers flit here and there. Their larvae will soon feed on the foliage of these locusts.

A dead shrew reminds us of the energy requirements of all the creatures we see here today. The least shrew is Kansas' smallest mammal and has an unusually high rate of metabolism. In 24 hours it eats an amount of food equal to 60 to 100 percent of its body weight. While it prefers insects, earthworms, snails and carrion, it eats seeds and fruits in emergencies. These foods contain higher concentrations of energy than do leaves, stems and roots.

Near streams of the park, eastern cottonwoods easily reach 16 meters toward the sky.

The sand, however, seems unable to anchor these prairie giants against midwest winds. Several cottonwoods have just lain over, the intact roots of one side rising out of the sand.

I jump across the stream that meanders through the park. (There is a foot-bridge for the heavy-hearted.)

The buffalo currant is in full bloom, uncertain whether its blossoms should be yellow or red. They turn out mostly yellow.

In the open woods, several morels, common edible mushrooms, display their tall, deeply pitted caps. They are the most obvious decomposers in the park today. Their task of recycling the minerals of the dead to be used by the living is important to all creatures of the woods and prairies.

Another large cottonwood! It would take three or four adult humans to reach around its trunk. At its base lies another trunk ripped from the side of the first. The fallen trunk lies like a trough cradling its decayed heartwood which has become the seedbed for Virginia creeper and a few mulberry saplings. I wonder whether their roots will reach the ground before their cradle decays and leaves their roots to dry to their death.

Several scattered branches of dead trees lie on the ground, their surfaces covered with a dark green moss. Gary Merrill, a specialist in mosses, tells me there are 150 to 160 species of mosses in Kansas. What a rich biological heritage in a group of plants that receives so little attention.

As we leave the woods and enter the sand prairie, we hear the field sparrow's song: two whistles and an accelerating trill. The handsome faces of tiny field pansies dot the trail. And one more plant with yellow blossoms, yellow star grass.

The brochure enticing people to visit the park reveals that the prairie has an average of 18 new species in bloom each week. We'll take another "brief look" soon.

With the Natives at Red Rock Canyon

Several hours of travel across the rolling plains and farmlands of west central Oklahoma brought us to the abrupt edge of Red Rock Canyon. Here, protected from severe weather and prairie fires, was a long, narrow valley filled with rocky ledges and native trees that were rare on the surrounding plains. Comanche and Kickapoo Indians probably sought shelter, firewood and water here for winter encampments before Europeans invaded the land.

It was late April in 1969. With our 5- and 7-year-old daughters, we had come for a weekend of camping with white families from central Kansas, and Cheyenne families from Oklahoma. A fine opportunity for us to share, with our children, a cross-cultural experience including our respective ethnic foods.

While our children explored the canyon and climbed the rocky ledges, we shared our cultural backgrounds: Arapaho, Cheyenne and European. After Arapaho Arthur Sutton and Cheyenne Robert Standingwater shared their cultures, I, as a last-minute substitute, described our migration to these grasslands. I had begun my presentation by matter-of-factly mentioning the purchase of land from the railroad after which our ancestors had converted prairies into wheat fields.

"But," responded a white acquaintance in the audience, "from whom did the railroad get the land? To whom did the land really belong?"

I was embarrassed! I had conveniently begun my report after the invasion had taken place, after the land was blatantly stolen from the ancestors of our new Indian friends. I had ignored the gulf between the cultures of native tribes and our European ancestors. I had not mentioned the dozens of treaties broken by our White government and the humiliations Native Americans suffered at the hands of our kind. I had blocked from memory, if I knew at that time, the attitude expressed in my home county in Nebraska that local Indians were uncivilized savages unworthy of Christian concern.

Later, we heard the moving story of the deliberate, unprovoked massacre of Cheyenne men, women and children by the troops of Col. J.M. Chivington (an ordained minister) at Sand Creek in eastern Colorado in 1864 (Nov. 29). And of a similar attack in 1868 (Nov. 27) by troops led by then-Col. George Custer at western Oklahoma's Washita River following the

Medicine Lodge Peace Treaty. Among the survivors of the Sand Creek Massacre was the great great grandmother of Cheyenne Lawrence Hart, who told us the story.

In this quincentenary of Columbus' arrival in the New World, I think of what our celebration might mean to our friends at Red Rock Canyon. How can I celebrate an occasion that triggered a series of events that so adversely affected the ancestors of our own church brothers and sisters?

At least I can recognize what really took place. I can remember that Columbus sent thousands of "red-skinned slaves" back to Spain. That on the island where Columbus landed in 1492, forced labor was so brutal that by 1640, not a single Arawak remained alive. That by 1900, smallpox, alcohol, the elimination of wild bison and direct extermination reduced the Native American population from 10 million to one million. That our nation's leaders signed and then broke treaty after sacred treaty with Indian tribes.

Of course much of that history is not unique. When any nation, tribe or family practices violence, its acts are clothed in noble terms like Manifest Destiny, self-defense or a struggle for freedom. And the opposing nation, tribe or family is brutal, terrorist or savage. And all manner of immoral acts against them are justified. Today, by managing the news media, our leaders are still able to mold us into whatever they need to further their political ends.

Should we feel a residual responsibility for the injustices perpetrated by our race or our nation? Should we focus on this dark underside of our history? Can we in honesty ignore it?

One way to commemorate the 500th anniversary of the New World is to recognize the injustices we have heaped on Native Americans, and on Blacks and others, and then work for positive reconciliation.

Some years after the Red Rock Canyon experience, at a church conference, Cheyenne Sam Hart invited a mostly White audience to "Come waste time with us." Perhaps only through person-to-person relationships will the natives of American prairies, African river valleys and the farmlands of Europe heal the wounds that all of us are still so willing to inflict.

118

The Vultures of Middle Creek

Among the trees lining Middle Creek in Chase County stands a small limestone house long abandoned. Inside, a stairway along the south wall leads up to a single room. Its roof has collapsed and patches of grimy plaster cling to its walls. The floor is littered with the leaves of bur oak, pieces of broken plaster, and several large black feathers. In the debris in the southeast corner stand two turkey vulture chicks. They are clothed in long fuzzy down of sheep-wool white, their faces and beaks forming black masks. Off to the side is half an empty egg shell, off-white with dark brown blotches.

Son-in-law Tim and I move carefully to avoid disturbing the chicks. The adult vultures gliding above the shack of this late afternoon in early May might include the young birds' parents; they may not take kindly to intruders.

Turkey vultures are widespread in the Americas and not uncommon here along Middle Creek. They often congregate on the trees, fences, and raised gateways of this valley. In the mornings, they can be seen spreading their wings toward the sun.

An adult turkey vulture stands about 75 cm (30 in) high and has a wingspread of about two meters (72 in). Its naked, wrinkled, red head emerges from a turtle-neck sweater of black feathers.

The first term in the turkey vulture's technical name, *Cathartes aura*, is Latin for purifier, and describes its ecological niche as a scavenger. Even children know that vultures eat carrion, dead, decomposing flesh. They occasionally eat fresh snakes, rats, or other easily killed animals. The birds' lack of head feathers makes it easier to keep their heads free of carrion.

Vultures apparently both see and smell their carrion while in flight. Birds in general have a sense of vision superior to that of other animals. They can detect

119

direction, size, shape, color, three-dimensional depth, and motion to high degree.

By contrast, most birds have a poor sense of smell. Turkey vultures, however, have exceptionally large, well-innervated olfactory organs. Experiments suggest that their sense of smell is highly developed. In one experiment, researchers hid dead mammals completely from view. As soon as the carcasses produced odors of advanced decay, many vultures collected over the hidden carrion. The same research team found that a "well-exposed, properly-posed," stuffed mule deer was ignored. When a team of engineers placed ethyl mercaptan (the odorous substance in carrion) in a 42-mile gas pipeline to reveal leaks, the sites of escaping gas were located immediately by observing groups of turkey vultures above them.

While vultures appear clumsy on the ground, their graceful flight is enviable. They fly mostly by soaring. This means that they maintain or increase altitude without flapping their wings. They can do this by gliding in rising air currents. These currents may be updrafts resulting when prevailing winds approach and rise over an obstruction such as a hill or bluff. Or the updraft may be a thermal, a convection current resulting from uneven heating of air in contact with the land. The air over dark, bare fields heats more quickly than air over forests or lakes. As air warms, it expands and becomes less dense and rises above the cooler, denser air around it. Turkey vultures soar with a gentle rocking motion, their wings forming a very shallow V.

But these chicks are not ready to fly or even hunt carrion. During their eight- to ten-week life in the "nest," they will depend on their parents for food. The adults will carry food in their crops and regurgitate it for their chicks. I hope someday to witness this spectacle.

Life in Caves

In about 1930, residents of Texas' Hill Country northeast of San Antonio, stumbled onto a hole in the rocky surface near a natural bridge. The opening led into cracks, roughly hewn tunnels, and mud bottomed channels that suggested further exploration. Apparently the forces that dissolved the rock from under the bridge had also formed underground cavities.

In about 1960, further investigation revealed spectacular caverns complete with stalactite/stalagmite formations and the columns they form when they unite. By now, local land owners have developed the cave into the Natural Bridge Caverns. Our guide this afternoon is a high school boy.

As far as light reaches into the cave, there is evidence of early Native American presence; spear points, arrowheads, and skin scrapers, all made of flint. Deeper into the cave, deposits of bat guano (manure) suggest the presence of bats until possibly a thousand years ago when a cave-in may have excluded bats from the cave. Fossils found in the cave include the jaws of a black bear.

Following the recent installation of permanent lights, a few ferns have sprouted and now grow in the rich guano substrate. Our guide suggests that the ferns developed from spores left here by bats a thousand years ago and excited to growth by the energy emitted by the installed lights. Perhaps more likely, the fern spores were introduced by visitors to the cave in more recent times.

Tumbling Creek Cave in the Missouri Ozarks is another cave with a food chain that involves guano. The summer colony of 150,000 gray bats inhabiting this cave eats an estimated half ton of insects each night. This generates over 100 kg (several hundred pounds) of guano which continues a food chain for over 100 species of creatures, according to biologist Cathy Aley. The over 600-meter (2,100-ft) trail passing through the cave illuminated only by our flashlights reveals fungi, fungus gnats, springtails, pseudo-scorpions, salamanders, pickerel frogs, and bats. Cathy recognizes several species of fungi growing on the guano. She is able to estimate the age of the guano deposit by the dominant species. Fungus gnats and many springtails feed primarily on these fungi and bacteria. The gnats and springtails, in turn, are eaten by larger insects which supply nutrients for hungry salamanders and frogs. These amphibians also eat the fungus gnats directly. And the frogs get other foods from the underground stream that parallels the trail.

This food chain, of course, begins outside the cave. The guano originates as insect tissue eaten by bats. Carnivorous insects devour herbivorous insects which graze or suck on plants. And the plants derive their energy for photosynthesis from the sun. Even the creatures living in the deep darkness of a cave depend, ultimately, on energy from the sun.

About 80 percent of Tumbling Creek Cave is off-limits for most human visitors to protect the cave and its natural inhabitants. Visitors at Natural Bridge Caverns are cautioned against even touching various observed structures. Touching a stalactite, for instance, can deposit body oils on its surface and cause it to repel water and alter the deposition of minerals. This is an example in which a trifling act causes significant, unintentional effects.

At Tumbling Creek, underground tours are preceded by a surface tour. Surface features such as the oak-hickory community, north/south slopes, sinkholes, and losing stream segments are observed and their effect on subsurface conditions are described by Tom Aley. He is a consultant on underground pollution and resource management problems in cave regions.

It is clear that surface waters supply the underground stream here. And bats carry their wastes into the cave projecting the outdoor food chain underground to supply nutrients to the cave food chain.

Clearly, a cave's inhabitants are as dependent on climate, geology, and the sun as we surface dwellers are. And the increasing dangers of polluting our groundwater supply makes spelunking (cave exploration) a very practical matter.

Tragedy Along the South Ninnescah

A shining ribbon of water curves among the shifting sandbars of the South Ninnescah River. A great blue heron stands knee-deep in water nabbing occasional fish for a meal. Scattered willows extend their limbs out over the river. Upstream stand a few cottonwoods, their leaves rippling in the breeze.

This tranquil scene suggests none of the drama played out here nearly 90 years ago when Herman and Martha Blumanhourst and their eight children were struck with the dreaded diphtheria.

Herman, born in Ohio in 1857, had settled on a claim in Kingman County. Martha was born in Illinois in 1874 to Mennonites William and Elizabeth Shrock and came with them to Kansas as a child. William traveled over Kingman County peddling pots, pans, and other household wares from his covered wagon. The sounds of those clanging kettles would announce the arrival of "Tinkler."

In 1888, Herman, age 31, and Martha, age 14, were married and soon settled in a three-room house along the South Ninnescah River on or near the present site of Camp Mennoscah, southwest of Murdock. By the onset of the dreaded disease in 1905, they had given birth to nine children, the second of whom died in infancy.

The physician called to the Blumanhourst home found "diphtheria in its worst form and the eldest daughter (Rosetta) to be in a horrible shape..." So reported the *Kingman Leader-Courier.*

Diphtheria is caused by bacteria which form a membrane in the throat and nasal passages that obstructs the breathing of its victims. The bacteria also produce a toxin which the blood distributes to all body tissues.

To prevent the spread of the disease to other families, the Blumanhoursts were placed under strict quarantine. Their bedding and clothing were burned and Kingman churches supplied fresh replacements. Food appeared from anonymous donors.

By 1890 an effective diphtheria antitoxin had been developed and Maudie, the sixth child, remembers getting frequent shots during the course of the disease.

But in spite of efforts to control the disease, 16-year-old Rosetta died on 16 January 1906. Her body was taken to the Belmont cemetery by wagon at night to avoid meeting people and further spreading the disease. The gloves and ropes used to lower the casket into the grave were buried with the body.

Before the burial, her sister Maudie recalls viewing the body. The experience gave her the strange feeling of an evil presence. Creatures who are among the smallest in nature had snuffed out the life of her sister.

Maudie remembers the deep loneliness the family felt during the absence of personal contact with other people. During this time of deep personal grief, neighbors and friends were unable to convey their sympathies. "Everyone was scared to death (of us)."

The intensity of their fear is illustrated by the unconfirmed story Lillian Blumanhourst Wineinger later told her children. Some individuals in the community, she understood, were ready to destroy the diseased family and burn the house if recovery wasn't evident by a given deadline. Lillian was born three years after the disease swept through the household.

As their health was being restored, precautions continued. The family's clothes were boiled in a large butchering kettle out in the orchard. The house was fumigated while the family lived in a tent. Maudie remembers the fumigant seeping from the doors and windows of the house.

Two more children were born to Herman and Martha, making a total of 11. Maudie Blumanhourst Ravenstein of Lindsborg, born in 1899, is the only surviving child.

Herman died in 1918 from wounds sustained from a kicking horse. He was large and tall and "worked himself to death," according to Maudie. After Rosetta's death he purchased a quarter section of land two miles west of the riverside claim. The three-room house near the river was allowed to disintegrate.

Martha lived until 1964 and is remembered as a mild-mannered, caring and compassionate woman with total devotion to her family. She is described as a saint, unconcerned about worldly things.

While the Ninnescah River episode was not a common topic of conversation in the family, grandson Earl Wineinger recalls his aunts weeping at family gatherings as they remembered, among themselves, those events that so devastated their family.

Today, wheat fields surround the Greenwood Cemetery 2.5 miles north of Belmont. Along the west fence are six catalpa trees casting their afternoon shade on the cemetery. Amid the red cedars and gravestones are the burial sites of Blumanhoursts, Shrocks, and other families of the community. Near the center stands a marble stone that says simply:

HARMAN H.
BLUMANHOURST
DEC 12, 1856
MAY 16, 1918
WIFE MARTHA
MAY 8, 1874
MAY 17, 1964

Nearby stands another, much taller stone that says:

ROSETTA
DAU OF
H.H. & M.
BLUMANHOURST
BORN
MAR 25, 1890
DIED
JAN 16, 1906
————
OUR LOVED ONE
AT REST

How little these headstones tell about the lives they memorialize. Do these stones withhold other dramas in the lives of these prairie people? (Gale D. Beck of Iola, Kansas, and Joyce Shields of Salina, Kansas, also contributed to this account.)

The Butterfly Milkweed

The clump of bright orange flowers among the lush prairie grasses in the Flint Hills demanded our immediate attention. In spite of our pressing schedule, Elaine and I stopped to take a closer look.

The flowers were clearly those of a milkweed. But orange? This is my first recollection of the blossoms that ecologist David Costello considered "among the most brilliant flowers in America." We were experiencing the butterfly milkweed.

The time was late May of 1955 in Chase County. In June of 1957 we saw similar plants near Medora in Reno County, this time with yellow flowers. And in August of that year, we saw the distinctly reddish-orange flowers north of Admire in Lyon County. Could it be that flower color in butterfly milkweed was dependent on soil type?

I discussed the possibility with botanist Ronald McGregor at Lawrence. He reported that Robert Woodson, herbarium curator at the Missouri Botanical Garden, was working on the question of color differences in this species. He had, in fact, collected plants of various flower colors into his home garden in St. Louis. In spite of identical environment, the variations in flower color persisted.

Butterfly milkweed is a familiar sight in much of the southeastern half of the United States where there is at least 50 cm of rainfall annually. This includes the eastern two-thirds of Kansas.

Woodson's extensive observations suggested an interesting pattern in color variation within its range. The red-orange color predominates in northeastern Missouri. From that center, yellow increases in frequency in all directions. The background pigments in all these flowers are the yellow carotinoids. Superimposed over the yellow is red anthocyanin, its amount determined by heredity.

Flower color and fragrant nectar join to attract insect pollinators and non-pollinators alike. The erect hoods of the milkweed flower are parts of the male stamens and contain the nectar which attracts insects. Frequent visitors are butterflies some of whom have eyes that are highly sensitive to reddish colors. (Butterflies may be the only insects that can see red.)

Plains Indians made some use of butterfly milkweed as food. The Sioux of the upper Platte River prepared sugar from the flowers and ate young seed pods. Roots were boiled and eaten in the northeastern U.S. Tender shoots were cooked and eaten like asparagus. Special treatment was probably necessary before eating any milkweed species as they are all considered to contain poisonous alkaloids.

This species was more widely used medicinally than any other milkweeds. It was used by Indians and pioneer doctors alike. The dried roots were listed in the U.S. Pharmacopoeia (1820-1905) and the National Formulary (1916-1936) as useful in inducing perspiration and the discharge of phlegm from the lungs. In larger doses it was suggested as a laxative and to induce vomiting.

The roots whether raw, cooked, dried, powdered, or chewed, were used for many additional ailments. These included dysentery, pneumonia, poisoning, colic, hemorrhage, rheumatism and pleurisy. "Pleurisy root" became one of its common names. Pleurisy root was one of the ingredients of a remedy popular in the late 19th and early 20th centuries. Known as Lydia E. Pinkham's Vegetable Compound, it was claimed as a cure for female ailments of all descriptions.

The official name of this prairie beauty is *Asclepias tuberosa* for the Greek god of healing, Asklepios, and the enlarged root which resembles a tuber.

Two more comments. This milkweed lacks the milky latex found in other milkweeds. And this milkweed is not a weed as it does not grow primarily in disturbed soil.

Chigger Mites

The striking orange-red blossoms of butterfly milkweed interrupted my trip through Chase County Flint Hills. I stopped to photograph some especially beautiful clusters and went on my way. By the next day I felt that I had encountered more than pretty flowers. The itching welts of chigger bites began to appear.

Kansans have learned to expect encounters with chiggers between June and September.

Chiggers, or chigger mites, are relatives of spiders and ticks. The most common pest chigger in the United States and in Kansas is *Eutrombicula alfreddugesi* found in scattered localities all across the contiguous 48 of the United States and into South America. Only this species of the 46 found in Kansas is particularly bothersome to humankind. And it is only the larval stage that is responsible for human discomfort. In Kansas, the larvae first appear in late May, increase in numbers until July, and mostly disappear by early November.

Chiggers do not burrow into the human skin and suck blood. They merely insert mouth parts into the skin and become firmly attached. They then inject protein-digesting enzymes which destroy cells around the bite. The enzymes also cause the host tissue to produce increased amounts of body fluids. The cells around the bite harden and form a tube which functions like a drinking straw through which the chigger drinks the host's body fluids and the digested skin cells. When the larva is filled, it drops off, if not previously removed by scratching.

The persistent itch and swelling of the bite are probably allergic reactions to the digestive fluid. The itching begins several hours after the insertion of mouth parts and may continue for several weeks. These reactions occur whether the chigger remains attached or is scratched off.

The site chosen by chiggers as they ascend the human body is often moist skin or areas where clothing fits tightly against the skin. The bases of hairs, the armpits, the groin and areas under waistbands or tops of socks are favored feeding places.

The life cycle of *Eutrombicula alfreddugesi* takes 55 to 68 days. About a week after becoming adults, female chigger mites begin laying eggs. They need not have had contact with a male to produce fertile eggs. The males scatter short, hair-like filaments with tiny containers of seminal fluid on the ground. Females walking by later pick these containers off the filaments with the genital region of their bodies. Fertilization of the eggs follows entry of the fluid. When the environmental temperature is suitable, the female begins laying its orange eggs, singly, on the surface of moist soil. She may lay up to seven eggs per day as long as conditions are favorable. After four to six days, each egg converts into a "second egg" which remains inactive for another week. Then the larva emerges as a six-legged creature, ready to feed.

The larva climbs a blade of grass, a bush, or anything that a food-providing host might brush against. It may wait as long as two weeks, without feeding, before a host appears. A variety of animals including birds, toads, snakes, rodents, and humans serve as hosts for various chigger species. As a suitable host brushes by, the larval chigger climbs on and searches for a desirable spot to feed. Human hosts usually end the chigger life cycle at this point by crushing or scratching off the larva. The feeding may take only one day or last a month. But each larva feeds only once. The engorged larva then drops to the ground and burrows into the soil.

After a week of inactivity, the larval skin is shed and the eight-legged nymph emerges. The bright red nymph lives in the upper soil layers feeding on insect eggs, immature insects and other small soil animals. Like the adult, the chigger nymph does not attack vertebrates.

After another week of inactivity the nymph's skin is shed and the bright red adult emerges. It has only eight legs and is about one millimeter long, clearly visible to the naked eye. It lives on moist soil, in the upper layers of dry soil, in leaf mold, under logs, or in clumps of grass. Its diet is the same as that of the nymph. If winter intervenes, the adult survives in a dormant state.

Chigger mites in the United States are not known to transmit disease-producing organisms that affect humans. But to avoid secondary infections from scratching, one can apply local antiseptics to the welts. If one encounters an infested area and has no repellents, several high-lather baths, each followed by rinsing, may prevent bites if taken soon enough.

The natural histories of chiggers and several other prairie creatures have been studied by the State Biological Survey of Kansas which makes the information available to interested persons. Edward Martinko of the Survey provided most of the information for this report.

Marijuana and Cotton

"Can you identify marijuana for us?" The call came from a local police officer during the early 1970s.

I recalled my childhood in Nebraska when we often crossed a neighbor's pasture on our way to Lonesome Ridge School. Some years, the marijuana growing there among the weeds along the creek was twice as tall as me. My older brothers knew it was marijuana, or hemp, and that the long tough fibers in its outer stem were used in making rope and twine. And that its leaves and green flowers yielded substances long used as hallucinogens. They could not have known that the active ingredient in marijuana, tetrahydrocannabinol, prevents transmission of those nerve impulses which coordinate movement and store memory.

Hemp was introduced to the Great Plains in the latter half of the 19th century as a field crop. (The *sativa* in hemp's technical name, *Cannabis sativa*, is Latin for "that which is sown.") But it had often escaped and grew well without cultivation.

The officer brought the mysterious plant potted in a one-gallon can. It had been discovered with others, also in cans, alongside a country road by a road maintenance man. He noticed that the plants were being watered regularly, leading to suspicion of illegal drug activity.

I knew immediately that the plant was not marijuana but looked a lot like a cotton plant. But the only personal photographs of cotton plants I had were one of a cotton boll in a Reno County garden and another of a cotton blossom taken in the flowerbed of the nuclear reactor center at the University of Kansas. As the plant was not yet in its flowering stage, I needed better pictures of cotton leaves.

I showed the plant to Sol Loewen, then Tabor College biologist. He, too, was uncertain of its identity.

The next morning, I took the plant to our high school's agriculture department. Teacher Truman Diener might have some good pictures of cotton leaves. There I interrupted Truman's conversation with a visiting agriculturalist from the African country of Uganda. The African immediately recognized the plant as cotton and I so informed the police.

Meanwhile, I was embarrassed by my inability to recognize the world's number one fiber plant. As far back as 8000 years, the Aztec Indians grew cotton for textile purposes in Mexico. And a host of economic and social problems of the past 300 years have revolved around this popular fiber; slavery and the U.S. Civil War, to name a few. Biologists should recognize it!

But the question remained, why plant cotton in cans and place them along country roads?

Sunday afternoon, while bicycling with our pre-teen-aged daughter Lisa, I decided to take a detour to report the identification to Sol Loewen. "Have you seen today's *Hutchinson News*," he asked. He brought the newspaper to the door for a quick skim. Apparently the drama being played out here had also taken place, with variations, in other Kansas counties. People found groups of plants in cans along country roads, and the plants were being tended, their unknown identity raising suspicions of illegal drug activity. Some sheriffs buried the suspicious plants.

The *Hutchinson News* story explained the mystery. Agriculturalists were investigating the possible presence and activity of the cotton boll weevil in southcentral Kansas by placing cotton plants in various locations. Their mistake, said the newswriter, was their failure to inform appropriate people and therefore avoid destruction of the plants by the unknowing public with the consequent disruption of the investigation.

Steve Tonn, local agricultural extension agent, reports that Kansas winters are probably too severe for the cotton boll weevil.

Cotton and marijuana are just two examples of plants that have long interacted with the social and economic life of the human animal.

Mutiny on the Plains

Kevin should have been attending his class; instead, he was running across the shortgrass prairie away from camp where classes were in session. I knew he had some difficulty adjusting to camp conditions, so I watched until he disappeared over the hill. With no help in sight, I followed at a distance, hoping that either fear or fatigue would turn him back without his knowledge of my pursuit.

The camp was on the Bar HL Ranch about 11 miles north of Liberal in southwest

Kansas. The Liberal and Turpin (Oklahoma) Mennonite Churches co-sponsored the summer day camp June 7-11 in 1971. In addition to their own children, they enrolled others from the northeast quarter of the city, children with limited opportunities. Each day, two buses transported the children from Liberal out to the ranch for classes and recreation. In late afternoon, they were returned to their homes. Elaine had been asked to assist with music activities. I was assigned to lead nature hikes.

During early morning classes, I scouted the area, planning nature activities for late morning sessions. The ranch reached north from the tree-lined Cimarron River. Most of the area was covered with short prairie grasses and other scattered perennial plants characteristic of this often parched land where evaporation rate is high and precipitation averages 48 cm (19 in) per year. We saw the handsome tansy aster with its purple rays surrounding a golden disk, and the oval-leaf bladderpod with its yellow blossoms about to mature into spherical capsules. We observed the yellow-flowered Rocky Mountain zinnia. We admired the prairie coneflower with purplish-brown disk flowers covering a tall column usually surrounded at its base with yellow rays, but here with striking purplish-brown ones instead. The dry stalks of last year's sand lilies up to a meter tall were everywhere, bearing cylindrical fruits. But I didn't recognize them until we saw the dried stalks associated with new growth later in August in Kingman County. Its new stalks bore sharply toothed leaves in late summer and handsome, cream-colored flowers. The aptly named Indianblanket flowers brightened the prairie scene.

Along the sandy river was the meter-high willow baccharis, not to bloom until August. There were cottonwoods of various ages. Beaver trails led from dozens of smaller cottonwood stumps to the river bank where branches were dropped into the water. Woven into the emerging aquatic vegetation were the nests of redwings. Catching tadpoles was a favorite activity for the kids. We found a small western spiny softshell turtle which can remove dissolved oxygen from water through membranes lining its mouth. It can stay underwater for a long time.

I guided the kids around a few marijuana plants to avoid leading them into temptation.

Where the woods met the open prairie, I was startled one morning by the sudden rushing of a wild turkey. Its ground nest of dry tree leaves held five off-white eggs covered with brown specks. Without disturbing the nest, it became one stop on that morning's hike.

Camp director Bill Stucky removed an owl chick from its stick nest to share it with the kids.

That this first-hand experience with the prairie and its creatures was important for the children was made clear one morning as our bus crossed the Cimarron. Having heard someone refer to the river below the bridge, a young girl remarked, "So that's a river!"

Tasty noon meals were prepared by church ladies. Occasional breaks included popcorn in a huge iron kettle over a campfire. When popcorn kernels are heated, the water inside the starch is hot enough to vaporize but it doesn't have room to do so. When the hull finally ruptures and decreases the external pressure, the internal moisture expands suddenly, exploding the starch to 30 times its original size. Those dancing white fluffs in the kettle reminded me of the bustle of activities designed to enrich the lives of these children.

But in spite of this flurry of camp activity, Kevin was trying to escape. As he alternately walked and ran, I tried to keep up with him without his seeing me. But there are few places to hide in the short grass prairie and it was all I could do to keep up. I had to think of a former student who claimed he chased jackrabbits until they stopped from exhaustion and then picked them up. I wasn't sure which of us would collapse first.

By now we were beyond Bar HL property. I learned later that the owner of this property had little sympathy for trespassers. And he had weapons with which he was willing to express his views.

A cloud of dust up the ranch road brought hope. It was Bill running a camp errand. From his perch in the van, he could see both Kevin and me. By now Kevin was not hard to convince that the attempt to escape was futile.

Kevin was lucky that he hadn't tried to escape in a dense forest. I was lucky, too.

The Poor Farm Cemetery

The clear whistle of a cardinal and the bubbling song of a western meadowlark greet me as I step through the gate into the cemetery of the old county poor farm. Among the mowed prairie grasses are 30 grave stones, standing at attention in several incomplete rows. Each stone is graced with fading plastic flowers.

Some old cemeteries in the Midwest are relics of native prairie and provide a hint of the original vegetation in the area. But here the native grasses are accompanied by black medic, ironweed, horsenettle, bindweed, cheat, and nut-grass. This mixture of native and introduced species suggests that the land was tilled before the bodies of the poor were planted here. Or frequent short mowing may have destroyed some of the tall prairie grasses.

A black swallowtail butterfly provides a momentary interruption as I read names on the grave markers. Each marker, except two, bears only the name of the deceased: "Bacilo Vazquez," "Percy A. McCousland," and on a stone adorned with poison ivy, "B. Eier." What appears to be the most recently placed stone bears both name and date: "William T. Moody, 1857-1938."

But the stone that really commands my attention is that in the northwest corner under a shrubby American elm. The words inscribed are simply, "Negro Boy." We can only wonder about the circumstances surrounding his life: name, parents, age, cause of death. Nobody knew even his name?

Hundreds of grasshopper nymphs jump, then rain back to the ground as I walk back toward the gate. A black field cricket backs into its hole as I pass. A spider scampers into a crack in the soil. Nearby is what appears to be the burrow of a tube-dwelling spider. Its 12-mm rim extends only a millimeter above the soil surface. A redwing's gurgling *konk-la-ree* echoes through the shrubbery.

Near the elm that casts an afternoon shadow on the Negro boy's grave is another shrub elm that holds a loosely constructed nest of twigs and stems. Less than a meter above the ground, the nest cradles two brown-blotched eggs. The dawn of new life so close to a plot dedicated to the dead! Life and death are never far apart.

Surrounding the cemetery is a shrub community of elms and mulberries. The space between shrubs is filled with poison hemlock, ironweed, and common milkweed. A brown thrasher glides silently through the brush.

Congregating on the white blossoms of poison hemlock are red-brown soldier beetles. These plant feeders are common in this area, according to Tabor College entomologist Richard Wall.

The purple-pink blossoms of common milkweed attract a bewildering assortment of creatures. Both monarch and silvery crescent butterflies flit from one flower cluster to the next. Arogos skippers crawl among the flowers. A flower spider maneuvers a lifeless moth three times its length to the underside of a leaf. Last night's supper stop was fatal for the moth. A red milkweed beetle crawls across a flower. This species eats both flowers and leaves of the milkweed. The nymph of the predaceous wheel bug stumbles among the crowded flowers.

A hackberry butterfly lands on my pantleg. I coax it onto my thumb so I can admire the bold brown and white spots on its soft-orange wings. Also crawling up my pantleg are two female American dog ticks. These flattened bodies are common in Kansas. I scrape them off forcing them to await a more-willing host.

The froth of spittlebugs is prominent on a variety of plants here—dogbane, common milkweed, smooth brome, common ragweed, and ironweed. The females produce this bubbly mass to cover their eggs. Their nymphs also produce the froth which hides them and keeps them moist while they suck juices from their host plant. These insects are also called frog-hoppers because they hop from plant to plant rather than fly.

The large stone house, once the residential center of the county poor farm, still stands as a stark reminder that our earthly fortunes are ephemeral. In recent years, it was reconditioned to become "Stone Prairie," a conference and retreat center. If these stones could talk, what tales of anguish and delight they could share.

I hope "Negro Boy" experienced the peace of the prairie.

Spring Along Cedar Creek

About a mile straight south of Cedar Point is a grassed hillside sprinkled generously with flint rocks and myriads of wildflowers all abloom as the billowy clouds above compete for attention. The sky now adds distant rolling thunder to gain added attention. But the land and sky needn't compete; each scape has its own beauty. And together they present a scene of unsurpassed synergy of splendor.

The variety of bloomers is breath-taking. From here among the lush grasses, I see patches of cobaea pentstemon, plains yellow primrose, green antelopehorn, plains ragwort, blue wild indigo, fleabane daisy, St. John's-wort, old plainsman, yarrow, plains larkspur, rose verbena, and the tiny prairie blue-eyed grass. At the base of the hill and all along the road paralleling the tree-lined Cottonwood River are patches of blooming dogwood, elderberry, showy white evening primrose, foxtail barley, spiderwort, and the lacey-leaved poison hemlock.

A nighthawk takes flight silently as I approach her resting place. Without a formal nest, these goatsuckers lay eggs in gravelly places. In case she is caring for her young here, I avoid the area ahead by veering to the right. At dusk she will take to the air and forage for insects until dark.

From where Cedar Creek empties into the Cottonwood River, I follow the creek upstream. It is lined with giant trees; sycamores, elms, bur oaks, and green ash. Honey locusts, black willows, and false indigo occupy space in the more open areas. Hackberries are developing dark green fruits not yet ripe.

The forest understory is densely covered with waist-high nettles near the creek. Further back are occasional woodland ruellia and golden zizia in bloom, plus pokeberry, poison ivy, and violets.

Recent flooding in this wooded bottomland has left debris as high in the trees as I can reach. Some leaves of hackberries and oaks appear to have been adversely affected; they have shrivelled where they have been submerged in flood waters.

My hero along Cedar Creek today is an old bur oak at the margin of the floodplain. It has lost its soil cover two-thirds of the way around its base and as deep as I am tall. The exposed roots, some as big as my leg, have grown straight down into the ground. To have withstood the rush of flood waters this spring with no apparent wavering of posture suggests roots that penetrate to great depths. This oak is a sermon about deep roots.

And the beauty of that flowering prairie hillside will long linger in the memory of this prairie wanderer. It is a parable of new beginnings.

Selected References

Alexander, R. McNeill. 1974. The Invertebrates. Cambridge University Press, Cambridge.

Allen, Durward L. 1967. The Life of Prairies and Plains. McGraw Hill, New York.

Bailey, Virleen. 1985. Kansas mustelids. The Kansas School Naturalist 31(4):3-15.

Bare, Janét E. 1979. Wildflowers and Weeds of Kansas. Regents Press of Kansas, Lawrence.

Barkley, T. M. 1965. J. B. Norton's grass investigation trip through central Kansas in 1898. Transactions of the Kansas Academy of Science 68(3):363-383.

Bates, Marston. 1960. The Forest and the Sea. New American Library, New York.

Bee, James W., Gregory E. Glass, Robert S. Hoffman, and Robert R. Patterson. 1981. Mammals in Kansas. University of Kansas Museum of Natural History Public Education Series No. 7.

Breukelman, John. 1973. Nature poetry. The Kansas School Naturalist 20(2):11.

Collins, Joseph T. 1982. Amphibians and reptiles in Kansas. Second Edition. University of Kansas Museum of Natural History Public Education Series No. 8.

_____, (ed.). 1985. Natural Kansas. University Press of Kansas, Lawrence.

_____, (ed.). 1991. Kansas Wildlife. University Press of Kansas, Lawrence.

Costello, David. 1969. The Prairie World. University of Minnesota Press, Minneapolis.

Curry-Lindahl, Kai. 1981. Wildlife of the Prairies and Plains. Harry N. Abrams, Inc., New York.

Drumm, Stella M., ed. 1975. Down the Santa Fe Trail and into Mexico: The Diary of Susan Shelby Magoffin, 1846-1847. William Gannon, Santa Fe, New Mexico.

Ehrlich, Paul R., David S. Dobkin, and Darryl Wheye. 1988. The Birder's Handbook. Simon and Schuster, New York.

Emory, W. H. 1848. Notes of a Military Reconnaissance from Fort Leavenworth, in Missouri to San Diego, in California including parts of Arkansas, Del Norte, and Gila Rivers. Senate Ex. Doc. No. 7, 30th Congress, 1st Session. Includes notes of Lt. J. W. Abert.

Gates, Dell E., and Leroy L. Peters. 1962. Insects in Kansas. Second Edition. Kansas State University Cooperative Extension Service Publication.

Gilmore, Melvin. 1977. Uses of Plants by the Indians of the Missouri River Region. Universtiy of Nebraska Press, Lincoln. First presented as author's thesis 1914.

Goodrich, Arthur L., Jr. 1946. Birds in Kansas. Report of the Kansas State Board of Agriculture, Topeka.

Great Plains Flora Association. 1986. Flora of the Great Plains. T. M. Barkley (ed.), University Press of Kansas, Lawrence.

Hall, E. Raymond. 1955. Handbook of mammals of Kansas. University of Kansas Museum of Natural History Miscellaneous Publication No. 7.

Heat-Moon, William Least. 1991. PrairyErth, a Deep Map. Houghton Mifflin, Boston.

Heitzman, J. Richard, and Joan E. Heitzman. 1987. Butterflies and Moths of Missouri. Missouri Department of Conservation, Jefferson City.

Horn, Bruce, Richard Kay, and Dean Abel. 1993. A Guide to Kansas Mushrooms. University Press of Kansas, Lawrence.

Jantzen, Paul G. 1960. The ecology of a boggy marsh in Stafford County, Kansas. Emporia State Research Studies. 9(2):1-46.

Kay, James S. 1982. Field Guide to Missouri Ferns. Missouri Department of Conservation, Jefferson City.

Kaplan, Beverly S. 1971. Daniel and Agnes Freeman, Homesteaders. Johnsen Publishing Co., Lincoln.

Kindscher, Kelly. 1987. Edible Wild Plants of the Prairie: An Ethnobotanical Guide. University Press of Kansas, Lawrence.

_____. 1992. Medicinal Wild Plants of the Prairie: An Ethnobotanical Guide. University Press of Kansas, Lawrence.

Martin, Alexander C., Herbert S. Zim, and Arnold L. Nelson. 1951. American Wildlife and Plants: A Guide to Wildlife Food Habits. McGraw-Hill Book Co., New York. Dover edition published in 1961, New York.

Martinko, Edward A. 1974. Chiggers in Kansas: their habits and effect on man. Bulletin No. 1f, State Biological Survey of Kansas.

Moore, Raymond C., C. G. Lalicker, and A. G. Fischer. 1952. Invertebrate Fossils. McGraw-Hill, New York.

O'Brien, Patricia J. 1984. Archeology in Kansas. University of Kansas Museum of Natural History Public Education Series No. 9.

Owensby, Clenton E. 1980. Kansas Prairie Wildflowers. Iowa State University Press, Ames.

Platt, Dwight R. 1974. Vascular plants of the Sand Prairie Natural History Reservation, Harvey County, Kansas. Transactions of the Kansas Academy of Science 76(1):51-73.

Reichman, O. J. 1987. Konza Prairie, A Tallgrass Natural History. University Press of Kansas, Lawrence.

Seton, Ernest Thompson. 1928. The Book of Woodcraft and Indian Lore. Vol. 4. Doubleday, Doran & Co., New York. First published 1912.

Stephens, H. A. 1969. Trees, Shrubs, and Woody Vines in Kansas. Regents Press of Kansas, Lawrence.

_____. 1980. Poisonous Plants of the Central United States. Regents Press of Kansas, Lawrence.

Thomas, Lisa Potter, and James R. Jackson. 1985. Walk Softly Upon the Earth, A Pictorial Field Guide to Missouri Mosses, Liverworts, and Lichens. Missouri Department of Conservation, Jefferson City.

Thompson, Max C., and Charles Ely. 1989. Birds in Kansas, Volume I. University of Kansas Museum of Natural History Public Education Series No. 11.

_____, 1992. Birds in Kansas, Volume II. University of Kansas Museum of Natural History Public Education Series No. 12.

Unrau, Ruth. 1968. Who Needs an Oil Well? Abingdon Press, New York.

Unrau, William E. 1991. Indians of Kansas. Kansas State Historical Society, Topeka.

Van Meter, Sandra. 1972. Marion County, Kansas, Past and Present. M. B. Publishing, Hillsboro, Kansas.

Vogel, Virgil J. 1970. American Indian Medicine. Ballantine Books, New York.

Waddington, Keith D. 1975. Ticks in Kansas: their habits and effect on man. Bulletin No. 2 of the State Biological Survey of Kansas.

Welty, Joel C. 1975. The Life of Birds. W. B. Saunders, Philadelphia.

Wilson, James S. 1963. Flowering plants of the Ross Natural History Reservation, Lyon and Chase Counties, Kansas. Emporia State Research Studies 11(4):1-91.

Zimmerman, John L. 1993. The Birds of Konza: The Avian Ecology of the Tallgrass Prairie. University Press of Kansas, Lawrence.